Fighting Spirit

The Life of Mario Spinelli

By
Suzanne M. Faed

Cover by Luke Buxton | www.lukebuxton.com
Front and rear cover photograph by Jessica Mill Photography

Dedication

This book, is, of course, dedicated to my Dad. Our relationship wasn't always easy, but neither was his life. We grew together over the years, and he showed me what it truly meant to stay strong in the midst of life's hurdles.

Thank you for always believing in me and showing me unconditional love. I will never forget the way you smiled and embraced me every time you saw me, even if the last time was only yesterday.

It was wonderful to be loved like that, and I will cherish it forever.

Contents

Prelude

When you look back on your life, what do you want to be remembered for? This is such a profound and personal question, yet one I asked my father on a perfectly normal summer's day. We were sitting at his kitchen table, with the breeze blowing through the door, and talking about his life. I am ashamed to say that, in all of my thirty-one years, this was the first time I had sat down and listened to his story. In my childhood, he was just my parent, not another person with thoughts and feelings of his own. In my egocentric and hormonal teens, he was a stranger, someone I didn't understand. Now as an adult, and a parent myself, I know him as not just my Dad, but also someone who I have come to truly value and appreciate.

Still, it wasn't until Dad started to become ill and was then diagnosed with cancer that I felt the urge to truly hear his story. Tragic news like this tends to send a jolt through you, making you remember how fragile life is. It also forces meaningful conversations to happen today because tomorrow is never guaranteed. So it was I listened to his story and so it was that his answer to that profound question brought this book into being.

Since Dad's youth, he was not blessed with good health. Illness plagued him, changed him and troubled him. It has defined most of his adult life, and yet, when I asked him how he wanted to be remembered, it wasn't for his sickness and how it shadowed his days, but instead for a simple, shared human desire: to be thought of as a normal person, one who had a kind heart and a caring nature. This need to be thought of as normal is one we can all identify with; we all want to belong and feel accepted by the people around us. Everyone has different definitions of 'normal' and the term can be quite subjective, but to Dad, normal meant loving others, showing kindness and respect, caring for other people's feelings and displaying friendship to those who mattered most. His heart belonged to his family; there was nothing more important to him than to be amongst loved ones.

This man, my Dad, had often been misunderstood. Years of taking various medications masked his true potential. His quirky sayings and ways of seeing things often disguised what lay beneath. So I realised it was up to me to unearth his story, to give his existence a voice, a chance to be heard and understood. His story is not an extraordinary one – a simple life filled with simple pleasures and plenty of trials in between. But to me, these types of stories are the most powerful, because they speak of the human journey. We are all on the same path, ultimately heading in the same direction, and all have experienced the uncontrollable see-saw that is life.

After I finished talking to my Dad about his life, he thanked me and said it felt good to talk about it, like a weight had been lifted from his shoulders. Sometimes, all it takes is for someone to stop and listen and take notice, as though the simple act of asking questions validates one's presence on this earth.

I am just sorry it took so long for me to ask.

1

Where it All Began

Cesario could hear his wife's screams in the next room, her desperate and pain-filled groans echoing throughout the house.

'Please!' she cried. 'Make it stop!'

But Cesario didn't go to her. There was only a thin wall separating him from her and yet he stood rooted to the spot. He couldn't go to her, and so he left her pain in the hands of the midwife, who was talking her through it. They had been in this situation before, five times in fact, and all Cesario could do was imagine the scene that was taking place – his wife pushing and panting, sweat dripping as the midwives prepared to deliver his baby. All he could do was pray that there would be no complications.

As it turned out, a healthy baby boy was delivered that day, the 3rd of May, 1951, in the town of Vasto, Italy. This atmospheric hilltop township is located on the Adriatic coast in the region of southern Abruzzo, and is almost directly opposite to Rome, the capital city of Italy.

It was the custom for women to deliver their babies at home with the help of midwives, and regardless of whether the woman wanted her husband by her side, he remained absent until the job was done and a cleanly wrapped baby could be handed over to meet its father. This was how Mario Spinelli entered the family, in a quaint farm house that was not their own and five siblings to share the space. Childbirth was not talked about with children, and so, when Mario was about to be born, the youngest children were told that their mother was not feeling well and had to go to her room. When she emerged with a baby and a slightly deflated belly, the children did not ask questions.

At the time of Mario's birth, he had four brothers and a sister. Francesco (Frank) the eldest, born in August, 1936; Giuseppina (Josephine) born in June, 1939; Alfredo (Alf) born in August, 1940; Armando born in August, 1942; Roberto (Robbie) born in June, 1945; then Mario in 1951, and finally, six years later, the youngest, Antonio (Tony) who was born in March, 1957.

Life was not easy for Mario's parents. Maria, Mario's mother, had a hard childhood; she was not sent to school because of her family's poverty, and because she was female meant she could be 'more useful' at home performing household duties. Her mother died from appendicitis when Maria was only eight years old, leaving her to look after the family. Eight years later, she lost her father to pneumonia. Life did not get any easier when she married Cesario – not long after their first-born arrived, Cesario left Italy and went to Africa for two years to attend military school. According to family recollections, Cesario achieved the position of Sergeant Major by the end of that time. With Italy's subsequent entry into World War II, Cesario would only be home for short periods of time for the next nine years. Almost each time he came home on leave, he and Maria would conceive another child. Before Cesario returned to War in 1941, Maria had given birth to the next two children, Giuseppina and Alfredo. Armando was born while Cesario was back at war, so it is fair to say Maria would have had her hands very full looking after the farm and all of the children.

But life was not any easier for Cesario, who was away from his family serving his country in the many theatres of war Italy found itself in.

When the war was finally over, Cesario returned home to his family, having felt such unspeakable heartache and uncertainty for many years. There was no time to wallow, though, as his family still needed to be fed and clothed, so he obtained a permanent job as a labourer on the Main Roads. At night, rest was still elusive, as he held a second job making olive oil for some extra income.

The land that Cesario and Maria farmed was not theirs, therefore three quarters of the produce they grew was paid to the landowners as rent. That only left a quarter for the family to survive on. They grew tobacco, grain, vegetables and various fruits, such as grapes, apples, pears and figs. They also kept chickens, rabbits and pigs, most of which ended up on their dinner plate, and some sheep, from which they obtained their milk. This was the situation that Cesario and Maria were in when Mario was born. The war, a still so recent memory and a farm that needed all hands on deck to ensure the family would have a meal on the table each night.

What follows is Mario's own brief recollections of his childhood in Italy.

I had nothing but respect and love for my parents and even at an early age I could recognise the sacrifices they made for their family in such difficult times. They lived a poor and simple life, with not much in the way of amenities to make life any easier or more enjoyable. My mother was a hardworking, strong, loving and caring woman. She never let us children see her emotions; rather she just got on with things and got the job done. For a woman who was unable to read or write and was not academic in any way, she managed to achieve what most would find a difficult challenge – raising a family, at times without her husband, whilst also running a farm and household.

My father had much the same qualities as my mother. I remember him as being strict, but I can recall that I was the only child in the family who never got smacked for being disobedient. I guess that was because I was well behaved. I used to love listening to the stories my father would tell of his own youth and things that had happened to his family. One such story involved Dad's father, Francesco Paolo Spinelli (the man who was my 'Nonno'), and how he came to claim his second wife. As the story goes, Nonno had his eyes on an eligible lady by the name of Rita. He had asked her to marry him a number of times already and he was getting impatient. He had four children at home who needed a mother, and he needed another wife as his first had died. In those days, if a man lost his wife, he would go in search of another to take her place. His proposition had been declined a number of times but he didn't give up, and eventually she accepted his offer. His insistence paid off and they ended up marrying and having seven children together.

Sadly, I never had any firm memories of my Nonno or Nonna, as they both died when I was very young. One thing I do recall, though, is a fleeting image of my Nonno hobbling along the road with his walking stick, carrying chestnuts and walnuts in his pocket as a treat for us, and me calling out, 'Here comes Nonno!'

When Mario was a baby and young child, his sister, Josephine, looked after him. She would change his nappies and feed him, as his mother was often busy working around the farm, and needed all the help she could get raising her children. All the siblings shared one room – being the only girl meant Josephine was lucky enough to have her own bed, but all the boys had to share one! The house was small, the main room being the kitchen, while the upstairs room was where Cesario and Maria slept. The children slept in the bedroom downstairs, on a mattress stuffed with corn leaves. The toilet was outside, and the family washed out in the open-air, using a round bowl filled with water, propped up by three skinny metal legs. The winters were bitterly cold, and the house wasn't any warmer.

I went to a government school in Vasto up until grade four and was, I think, a well-behaved boy because I loved school. My teacher had a soft spot for me. She loved me. She reckoned I was one of the best students and she used to look after me. Even when I left Italy, she told me to keep in touch. Of course, being young, I never did.

When I wasn't at school and was old enough to help around the house, my jobs involved cleaning the home and chopping wood. There was a well by the side of the house and I was expected to draw water from it, both for the family and for the landlord who lived next door. It used to annoy me because she, the landlord, would come over at lunchtime on a Sunday and say 'I want some water now!' So I had to go there and wind the thing up and pull the bucket of water up for her. I would also walk over to the landlord's house to polish her tiles and fix holes in the walls when they needed repairing, using flour paste. I didn't enjoy these jobs as I thought she was grumpy and mean. But I had no choice and I had been taught to respect my elders, so I kept my thoughts to myself and kept on working.

Coming from a traditional Italian family meant Mario and his siblings were raised as Roman Catholic. Every Sunday, the family would walk to church in the dark, their combined footsteps stirring up the dirt and puncturing the quiet that hung in the early morning air. When they arrived, Mario would leave his family, go and change into his robes and serve as an altar boy. He took this job very seriously and from an early age had a strong faith in God and the church. His father also did odd jobs for the church and kept the surrounding garden trim and tidy. As payment, the monks that worked at the church would send Mario to summer camp up in the mountains. He would be away for a month and participate in activities and prayer sessions. Mario enjoyed this time and found it to be a nice break from his daily life at home. Sometimes his mother would come and visit for a few days, and no doubt she found that time away to be a brief retreat and respite from her daily grind as well.

When Mario was about five years old, he had his tonsils removed. His brother, Robbie, had his taken out at the same time. Mario used to get frequent infections in his tonsils and so it was decided that removing them would fix the problem. Tonsillitis was a common condition, as was the decision to surgically remove them if infection was recurrent. What is unbelievable is the fact that Mario had his tonsils removed with no anaesthetic. It is hard to imagine the fear and pain that comes from a scenario like this, let alone the trauma inflicted upon a child that must have had lasting effects. As Mario sat in a chair, an apron covering his body to soak up the blood, the doctor placed a brace in Mario's mouth and then used a medical instrument to extract the tonsils from his throat. He had to open his mouth as wide as he could, and sit helplessly as the doctor pulled and yanked, screaming and coughing blood as the doctor rummaged inside his mouth. When the worst part was over, as Mario sat crying uncontrollably and calling for his mother, the doctor put some ice packs in Mario's mouth. Tears ran down Mario's face and mixed with the blood that dripped from his nose and lips. When the doctor had cleaned him up and controlled the bleeding, Mario was able to go to his mother and Robbie, who had been through the same ordeal. Mario left the doctor's, hoping to never see that man again, but he had to return a couple of weeks later so the doctor could check inside his mouth to see how it was healing. Sitting in the same chair he had been in only weeks before, his memory of writhing in agony at the doctor's mercy became too much, and as the doctor put his finger inside Mario's mouth, he bit down on the digital intruder. Shocked, the doctor hit Mario across the face, leaving a bruise as another reminder of what Mario had been through. He healed in time, but the memory of that procedure was still vivid in Mario's mind decades later. His hearing was also permanently damaged as a result of his tonsillectomy. From then on, he was partially deaf in both ears, creating more challenges as he grew up having to adjust to hearing the world at a muted volume.

After years of hard work and faced with a bleak future, Maria had urged Cesario to move to Australia as many people from the region seemed to be migrating there and prospering. When Mario was five, his brother, Frank, made the journey to that far away country in search of a better life. Alf followed when Mario was eight. The two brothers worked hard in Australia and once they had enough money to secure a house, Frank and Alf made a request for the rest of the family to join them. Once this was approved, preparations began to pack up the only life Mario had ever known and move to a country of which he knew very little. The future was uncertain, but a fresh start in Australia seemed more promising than their current life in Italy, so the family said goodbye to their hometown, and started their voyage towards a new life.

TOP LEFT: *Mario's parents, Maria and Cesario Spinelli.*

TOP RIGHT: *Mario's home in Vasto, Italy.*

ABOVE LEFT: *Family photo. From left, standing – Frank, Mario, Maria, Cesario, Josephine, Robbie. Kneeling – Alf, Armando, 1952.*

ABOVE RIGHT: *Mario washing outside the home, Italy.*

TOP LEFT: *Mario at his Holy Communion, 1959.*

TOP RIGHT: *Mario at 10 years of age, Vasto, June, 1961.*

ABOVE: *Passport photo – Tony, Mario, Maria. As minors, Tony and Mario had to appear on their mother's passport.*

2

Moving to Australia

On the 6th of September, 1961, Mario and his family left Vasto and two days later arrived in Naples. Here, they boarded the ship Flaminia, an old workhorse that had spent many years journeying migrants across the seas to better destinations. This journey to Fremantle, Western Australia, was to be the ship's last voyage and on her return to Italy she was scrapped.

Mario and his family would spend almost a month on board, surrounded by nothing but ocean and sky, the days and nights dragging. Mario spent most of the journey sick. He developed a cyst on his temple, which needed to be removed. The doctors sought Cesario's permission to do this, and once again Mario felt scared and helpless as they prepared to operate. This time, though, he was anaesthetised, but the method was traumatic and he screamed and fought until the drug overcame his body and he finally succumbed. Cesario stood outside, unable to help Mario. The doctors placed a mask over the boy's mouth and poured ether, a liquid that was used as an anaesthetic, as Mario cried and screamed, 'Help! Help! Help!'

Although, his screams meant that he inhaled the liquid

quicker, and in no time at all, he was asleep. When he woke up, the effects of the drug made his bones ache terribly, and it took him most of the trip to recover, only starting to feel better about a week before they arrived in Fremantle. English lessons were given on the ship to help prepare the passengers for their new country and Mario participated when he felt well enough.

Eventually, on the 3rd of October, 1961, the ship sailed into the port of Fremantle, and the relief of having arrived safely and completing the long and exhausting journey was overwhelming. Mario's sea legs were wobbly and weak as he stepped onto Australian soil for the first time. His brothers, Frank and Alf, were there to greet the family and take them to their new home in Bunbury, a small and quiet town about two hours drive south of Fremantle. The family's new residence in Bolton Street had been organised by Frank and Alf, who had bought the place from friends. The house was small and basic, not much of an upgrade from their former home in Italy. All the boys had to share one room again, but this time they had different beds. Josephine had her own room, but she didn't live at Bolton Street for long. While still in Italy she had been exchanging letters with a man called Guy, their long-distance relationship blossoming through their written words. The young couple met for the first time when the family arrived in Fremantle, and not long after, Guy and Josephine were married. Mario remembered the main benefit to him and the rest of his siblings was the freeing up of a room in the family home. The house had an outside toilet, but inside was an old-fashioned bath, which was filled with water that had been warmed with the wood fire water heater. This meant the family could at least bathe and clean themselves indoors, out of the elements. A most welcome improvement from their home in Italy.

Life couldn't have been more different to what Mario had

known back in the 'old country'. He could only communicate with his family and other Italian-speaking people, as he knew no English, apart from a few words he had learnt on the ship. His father found work on the railways and his mother stayed at home and raised the children. Mario was placed in a Grade Four class at St Mary's Catholic Primary School for the remaining few months of the school year. Mario was an easy target for the bullies in the class, who used his language barrier as an excuse to tease him. This didn't bother Mario and it didn't stop him from loving school. He had enjoyed school in Italy and that didn't change when he moved to Australia. He had a mind for education and he wasn't going to let the teasing squash his passion for learning. Mario certainly had no problem sticking up for himself and would often get into fights.

Especially with the 'wealthy kids'. Those 'stuck-up ones' who thought they were better than everyone else. Somehow, I avoided the cane but I remember the teacher used to use a long bamboo stick, long enough that she could still sit at her desk comfortably and simply aim it at the trouble-maker, whacking them across the arm or head or wherever it happened to land, no doubt hitting a few innocent victims on the way through.

There must have been something about Mario that the Australian teachers appreciated, because they loved the little Italian boy, just like his teacher had, all the way back home in Italy.

The following year, 1962, saw Mario start at a new school, Marist Brothers, and he stayed there until he finished his junior schooling, although he had to complete Grade Five twice, as the first time he struggled because of his language difficulties. That first year at Marist was difficult because Mario was still learning English, but after that, things became easier as he slowly became accustomed to the new way of speaking.

Mario enjoyed good health as a child in the bright, warm and agreeable climate of southwest Australia, and he liked playing tennis, football and handball at school.

In 1966, Mario started First Year High. He was able to choose elective subjects and he chose the courses that allowed him to work with his hands – metalwork, woodwork and technical drawing. He also chose to do elementary mathematics as he found that subject difficult, but without doubt his favourite subjects were metalwork and woodwork. The enjoyment of working with his hands was a revelation to him and set him on the path to his future career. As a teenager in the mid-sixties, Mario certainly wasn't what you would think of as stereotypical. He spent a lot of his free time studying in his room, sitting on a hard chair at a tiny desk, head bent over his books. His mother would often come in at 11:00pm with a cup of steaming coffee, when Mario's eyelids were starting to droop, and this coffee would be enough to keep him going for another couple of hours. A perfectionist, he cared passionately about achieving good results. It crushed him when he failed a test, even if only by one mark, a hard thing to accept when one is so focused on getting everything right. These disappointments he felt keenly and the stress they caused him was no doubt a precursor to the mental health problems that Mario would face in a few years' time.

He finished the Third Year of High School in 1968 and immediately applied for an apprenticeship at the Bunbury Power Station. He started with a three-month trial period and when that was over, he signed to accept a full apprenticeship with the company. This required him to attend the local Technical and Further Education institution, or TAFE, one day a week to undertake supplementary training to assist in completing the apprenticeship. These new studies would earn him a certificate in Fitting and Machining. The remainder of the week he would work at the power station. He also studied part-time at the local Bunbury Technical College, spending two to three nights a week learning Fourth and Fifth Year High School subjects. The apprenticeship took him four years to complete, and after that, he stayed on for three months, working as a fitter and turner. The duties included fixing faults and making replacement parts for the machines. Mario loved building and creating, from having ideas in his mind to seeing them come to fruition by the work of his hands.

He had a few close friends in high school, most of them Australian-born Italians, but when he left school and started a new chapter of his life, his friends did not stay in contact. He felt that they all betrayed him, by leaving him and his friendship behind. He was busy working, though, and didn't have the time to worry about it. To be fair, he also didn't make the effort to stay in touch either.

In 1970, Alf got married and stayed at the house on Bolton Street with his new wife, Teresa, while Mario, Tony, Robbie and Armando shifted with their parents to a new residence on Beach Road. Life seemed settled, but Mario wasn't to know what, or rather who, was about to come into his life.

TOP: *Flaminia, the ship that brought Mario and his family to Australia.*

ABOVE LEFT: *In the backyard of Bolton Street home – Mario and Tony, 1961.*

ABOVE RIGHT: *Junior School, Marist Brothers – Mario second row from top, third from left.*

ABOVE: In the lounge room of Bolton Street home –
Tony, Maria, Mario, 1964.

ABOVE: Many hours spent
studying at this desk, Bolton Street.

RIGHT: Mario being Naturalised
by Ernest Cosmo Manea, Mayor
of Bunbury, at Bunbury Council
Chambers, 21st January, 1968.

3

Dating Josephine

Mario was enjoying living in Australia. The family had come at the right time, the country was booming and opportunities were just around each corner. As a family they were making progress; the brothers built each other's houses with no outside help. Their sweat and hours of hard labour made homes that they would later be able to settle down in and start families of their own.

That seemed a far off prospect for the young Mario, but in 1971, when he was just twenty and had finished his apprenticeship, he met a girl called Josephine.

She was a secretary at an office and was only a few months younger than Mario. Through family connections, Mario had heard Josephine was single and a potential match. She lived in Fremantle with her parents, and one day opened the door to Mario and his mother, who had made the trip up to proposition Josephine to begin a courtship with Mario. She accepted but it soon became clear that it wasn't going to be a free and easy relationship; Josephine's mother chaperoned them whenever they went out together and they couldn't do anything on their own. Their outings consisted of visiting family, and other than that, they would stay at home, under the watchful eye of her mother. Mario wasn't allowed to sleep under her roof, not even in a separate room, so he slept at Connie's parents' house, which happened to be around the corner from Josephine.

Mario would work all week at home in Bunbury, then, as soon as he could get away on a Friday, he would drive to Fremantle to see Josephine. His heart would race as he drove along the old road in his battered car. He pictured her welcoming face and it was like a beacon guiding him to her. In the days before the freeways, the journey took him three hours but he was never deterred, even though it meant he could barely spend twenty minutes with her on a Friday evening. They would share as much time as possible on a Saturday, still under the watchful gaze of parents and then they would both attend mass together on Sunday mornings. Ironically, squeezed together on the pews of the chapel was often the closest they could come to one another throughout all their courtship.

As the year went on, Mario and Josephine's feelings became stronger for one another. With his courage gathered, Mario proposed. To his great relief she immediately said yes. So their courting turned into an engagement and invitations for their marriage were made, but Josephine's parents kept making excuses as to why these invitations were not being sent out. Mario's frustration and annoyance grew, as they continued to interfere with and dictate every detail. Eventually, the invitations were handed out to the family, and Josephine's parents put pressure on Mario to move to Fremantle. Mario had no desire to leave Bunbury and refused to give in to them. He bought a block in Bunbury, which angered her parents. This purchase of land proved that Mario was staying put, and his unwillingness to live in Fremantle was not well received. Josephine's parents cancelled the engagement, giving Mario the awkward job of taking back the invitations that had been sent out. It all ended abruptly, the severing of the relationship harsh and horrible, two years gone just like that. At that time, the focus was on settling down early and starting a family, and suddenly that prospect had been ripped away. Mario got into his car and drove back home on his own, the events replaying in his mind as his hands gripped the wheel and his head pounded in anger. He was extremely distressed, and as the distance stretched out, closing the end of the relationship and the possibility of marriage, the disappointment enveloped him and planted a seed within him. An unhealthy mix of emotions began to simmer; his hurt and humiliation would soon erupt, changing the course of his future and his mind.

He was so distressed; it was a miracle that Mario made it home safely. When he walked through the door his mother was there, and as soon as she saw the condition he was in, she was immediately concerned. While his face flushed and his hands shook, she asked him what had happened.

After he explained, she asked, 'How did you make it home in this state?'

'Saint Anthony brought me home.'

Worried by Mario's state of mind, she marched across the road to her son Frank's house to use the phone to call Josephine's mother.

'Mario's not well,' Maria said when the phone was answered. 'What did you do to my son?' she accused.

Josephine's mother said, 'We didn't do anything to him!'

The animosity ran down the line, these two protective mothers proving to be a dangerous combination. The conversation ended, and Maria was left to pick up the pieces of her son's broken heart, and as it seemed, his faltering mind.

Mario had left some of his belongings at Josephine's house, so not long after, he and his brothers took a trip up to Fremantle to retrieve his things. Where once he knocked on the door to eagerly ask for Josephine's hand, he now knocked to sheepishly ask for the return of the possessions that would erase him out of their lives for good. Her parents, being typically difficult, refused to give them back. Frustrated, the brothers went to the Police Station in the hope that they could help, but it was a dispute that they didn't need to be involved in, the officers telling them they would just have to convince them to give his stuff back. Eventually, Mario had his possessions returned and after that, they were out of his life for good.

He never spoke to Josephine again, but heard along the grapevine that she had moved on with her life, eventually marrying a man who ironically happened to be an old school friend of Mario's. Back then, he had lived not far from Mario. He would pick Mario up and drive him to school, and would then sit next to each other in class.

So with this prospect gone, Mario had to refocus and get on with his life. But the ending of this relationship may have triggered the beginning of something far worse. Maybe Mario was more affected by this than he let on and maybe this was just another contributor to the big problems he was about to face. Whatever it was, little did Mario know that these days would be the last of what he knew to be normal. Day by day, his reality was changing. His rational mind was slipping away and there was nothing he could do to stop it.

4

Diagnosed with Schizophrenia

In 1972, Mario left the Power Station to work at the Super-phosphate works in Picton. This company made fertiliser for farmers, and Mario worked as a fitter and turner, fixing machinery including belts, motors and conveyers.

As a young man, Mario was always working. He pushed himself too hard, not allowing any time for a social life. From the beginning of his apprenticeship, life was busy with limited free time and this impacted his mental health.

In 1973, when Mario was twenty-two, he began to feel seriously depressed. It started not long after he and Josephine went their separate ways, building up inside him until he could no longer contain it. Feelings were not something often spoken about in Mario's family and so he kept this burden to himself, afraid to admit weakness and ask for help. But as time went on, these feelings of depression started to consume him, turning him into a completely different person. It must be a scary and lonely circumstance, to feel yourself slipping away and to have absolutely no control over what was happening, too afraid to seek help, too afraid to let go, to let somebody in. Clinging helplessly to your sanity, thought by thought, until the new but strange thoughts that occupy your mind are considered truth. Until eventually, reality is blurred beyond recognition. So when Mario started hearing voices in his head, to him they were as audible and real as if there was someone sitting right beside him. His parents and brother, Tony, had returned to Italy for a visit, but the rest of his family could see the change in Mario. His brother, Alf, stepped in and practically carried him to their local General Practitioner. Mario couldn't understand why he needed to see a doctor and when he was questioned about the reason for his visit, he looked at the doctor with glazed eyes, and said, 'Oh God, let it be.' The stigma and negative perceptions attached to mental illness were very alive in society, so the doctor's approach to Mario's statement was to smack him across the face in the hope it would knock some sense back into him. He then gave Mario an injection to calm him down, before sending him to Sir Charles Gairdner Hospital in Perth where he stayed for the next couple of months. He became a guinea pig, his mental health questioned and tested, his responses closely examined, until the doctors were able to label him as a Schizophrenic. At first they thought Mario had suffered a nervous breakdown, but after these tests, they saw it was something more serious. When Mario had these Schizophrenic episodes, he would be completely overtaken by the voices in his head. He fully believed he could see God, and was having conversations with Him. He had visions of God's future plans, these spiritual experiences being seen as completely crazy to those who witnessed it, but to Mario it was all truth. He was amazed by a wall of stars; nothing was irrational or unbelievable when he was in this state. After these psychotic episodes, Mario would come crashing back to reality, his mood extremely low, and he would have to fight through the confusion and terror as his mind tried to grasp what he had just experienced.

Schizophrenia is marked by the disconnection between thoughts, feelings and actions. Unlike other illnesses this disease is not diagnosed through blood tests, biopsies or other measures. Instead, it is diagnosed by a full psychiatric assessment. A trained psychiatrist will ask about background information and assess a range of symptoms by asking questions that are designed to elicit key symptoms. There are two categories into which symptoms fall: positive and negative. Positive symptoms include delusions, hallucinations (these can be auditory, visual, olfactory, gustatory and somatic), and thought disorder. Negative symptoms include apathy, reductions in speech, blunted emotional responses, social withdrawal and reduced social performance.

Much of what we hear about Schizophrenia is false. Many people believe schizophrenics have split personality. This is not true. Schizophrenia means 'divided mind'. Schizophrenics are rarely dangerous or violent. Those being treated with Schizophrenia are no more violent than other members of society. Mental illnesses are not a form of intellectual disability or brain damage; they are illnesses like any other. There is still so much stigma surrounding mental illnesses and this is because many people are uninformed.

Unfortunately, Mario now had to learn how to live with this illness, to find a way to keep going with these voices in his head. The doctors put him on medication and when it seemed to be doing what it was supposed to and he was considered well enough to leave, the doctors discharged him. This visit to the psychiatric ward was just the beginning of many hospital stays over the coming years, the mental illness taking a hold of Mario's life and claiming more and more of the man he used to be.

He was forced to take a couple of months off work, needing that time to recover and recuperate and allow the medication to balance the chemicals in his brain so he could think clearly once again. Over the next few years, Mario went about life as best he could, taking his medication to keep the voices and visions away. He continued to work, his body still young enough to bounce back and continue with day-to-day life.

In 1975, Mario left the super works and started working at Laporte, which is now known as Cristal, in Australind, a fifteen-minute drive from Bunbury. He had applied for work at this company in March, but had been knocked back a few times. Then, four months later, he received a letter saying that a position was available. He began working there on the 21st July, 1975.

That year also saw Mario have a relapse with his Schizophrenia, his first episode since he became ill two years earlier. His parents and brother, Tony, were back in Italy at the time, on a three-month holiday. It was difficult for Mario, not having his parents there to support him. He was still in hospital when they returned, and Mario was relieved that they were now home to help him back to recovery. When he was well again he returned to his job at Laporte. He remained there until one day, in April 1976, he received a letter from the clerk at the Bunbury Power Station, where he had completed his apprenticeship, advising him that there was a position available. Mario gave a week's notice to his employer at Laporte and then began working at the place where he would spend the next seventeen years.

He applied the same dedication to his work as he had done with his study and earned a reputation as being very good at his job. He was very particular and would spend a long time on each project, making sure everything was faultless. This perfectionism, along with Mario's serious nature, was the reason why some of the workers took a dislike to him, picking on him and calling him names. It may have been a bit of jealousy between some of the workers and Mario because he was given the good jobs, leaving the undesirable work to those less competent. He did have a few good friends there, though, which made the bullying easier to endure. Ron Harrison, an electrical fitter, Albert Ceccato, a tradesman assistant, and Ron Leach, who was the foreman, saw in Mario what the others didn't, and respected the effort he put into his work. His brother, Armando, also worked at the Power Station, so Mario enjoyed working alongside his sibling too.

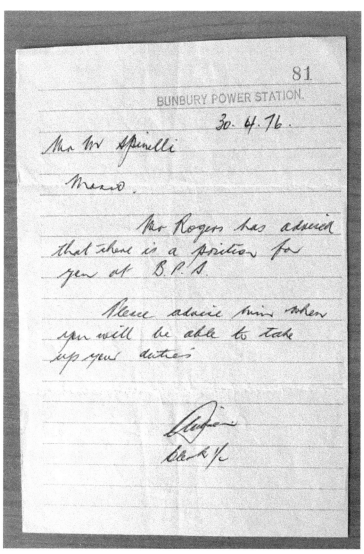

ABOVE: *The request letter that the Bunbury Power Station sent Mario, informing him of a position, April, 1976.*

5

Meeting and Marrying Maria

In 1978, when Mario was twenty-seven, he was introduced to an Italian girl by the name of Maria Timpani. He knew of Maria through family connections, she was the first cousin of his sister-in-law, Angie. Italians have a knack of finding out things through talk amongst family, so it was discovered that Maria happened to be an eligible eighteen-year-old who lived with her parents. On a cold day in July, Mario and his mother knocked on the door of Catena Timpani. The two mothers spoke and came to an arrangement. Maria was sitting in the kitchen by the wood stove, pretending to stoke the fire, but she was eavesdropping on the conversation that would determine her future. She had a week to think about whether she would like to start seeing Mario, a man she knew nothing about but had briefly met a number of years before. In 1973, when Maria was thirteen, she was in the bridal party of her cousin, Angie. Mario was also there, given it was his brother who was marrying Angie, but with the age difference and the fact he was still dating Josephine at the time, neither Mario nor Maria had much to do with each other. It would have been unbelievable if someone had predicted that their future spouse was only meters away. That this unfamiliar stranger, so close by, would be the person they would one day wake up beside. Like a tide that ebbs and flows, they were brought together, then pushed apart, and years would pass before they would see each other again.

At the time that they finally did meet, Mario was building a house. He had bought a block of land on Scott Crescent, in East Bunbury, and was spending weekends laying the foundations for his future home. He had the help of his father, who had been through a hip operation, but would still help out where he could and of course the rest of the brothers.

Mario had chosen a central location to build his house. The area was mostly established, with only a few empty blocks remaining on the street. The house next door, on the right, was a Police Department house. Its purpose was to accommodate local police officers and their families while they served their community, until they moved on to another posting. Across the road was a park, with shady trees and some basic play equipment and a phone booth. Behind the block, only a few streets away, was the Marist Brothers school. It would later become known as Bunbury Catholic College. The South Western Railway was also located close by, which allowed passengers to travel from Bunbury to Perth.

When Mario first started to build his house, he could only hope that he would find a wife. Just a year later, the house was complete and he had met and married Maria. Their courtship only lasted seven months. This courtship was much like when Mario was seeing Josephine, in that they were never allowed to go anywhere without a chaperone, even to church. Maria's father was extremely strict, and would not permit Maria to go anywhere with Mario on her own. One night, they went to the drive-in cinemas to watch Grease. It was a whole family affair, with nine people crammed into the one car. This date couldn't have been any more unromantic, with Maria's mother, father, sister and four brothers all taking up every inch of space and making for a very uncomfortable couple of hours.

The short courtship, along with the fact that they couldn't ever get a spare minute to themselves, meant that when the day came for them to be married, neither of them really knew who they were marrying. Those deep and meaningful conversations where couples get to know and understand one another were non-existent. They knew each other on a surface level, the things they could see and hear at the time carving an initial impression, but lacking the details that really connect a couple in love. So when Mario watched Maria walk down the aisle on the 24th February, 1979, there were things that still remained unspoken. When they exchanged their vows, promising to look after each other in sickness and in health, Mario had failed to tell Maria about a very important detail of his health. He had assumed that she knew already, because Bunbury was small and everyone knew each other's business, so surely Maria would have heard on the grapevine. But still, he chose not to speak of it and yet it was there, lying dormant, a side of Mario that hadn't been revealed to Maria, a side that would impact their marriage greatly.

After the wedding, they didn't have a honeymoon as we would recognise one today. Instead, they spent a couple of nights at the Mounts Bay Road Motel in Perth. From there, they went to Northam to stay with his sister, Josephine, and her husband, Guy, for a few nights. When they returned, they settled into their new home on Scott Crescent.

TOP: *At Robbie's wedding, where Mario stood behind Maria, his future spouse, unbeknownst to them. Maria in the middle, Mario standing behind at bridal table, 1973.*

ABOVE LEFT: *Mario and Maria at a friend's wedding, October, 1978.*

ABOVE RIGHT: *Mario and Maria's Engagement Party, 18th November, 1978.*

TOP: *The shed taking shape at Scott Crescent.*

ABOVE: *Spinelli Family, from left – Josephine, Maria, Cesario, Frank, Alf, Armando, Robbie, Mario and Tony, 1979.*

ABOVE: Mario and Maria's wedding day, 24ᵗʰ February, 1979.

Scan this QR code to watch a video of Mario & Maria's Engagement Party. Or visit:
www.suzifaed.com/engagement-party/

6

The Joy of New Life and the Sorrow of Death

Within the first few years of Mario and Maria's marriage, Mario had a second relapse, and the thing that hadn't been spoken about became glaringly obvious as the young wife watched her husband's mental health crumble. Maria could see that he was acting strangely so she took him to hospital, shocked and scared to be a witness to this illness. The relapse wasn't a major one, and after Mario's medications were adjusted, he began to get better. When he came home from hospital, Maria asked him why he had failed to tell her about his illness. He said that he thought she already knew. He was met with silence, and just as quickly as the conversation began, it was over. Feelings were hidden, resentments buried and thoughts concealed as they continued on with their life. They decided it was time to start a family and after a while of trying to conceive, Maria fell pregnant. In March, 1981, Mario's first-born son entered the world. After a long and exhausting labour, Matthew Stephen was finally born at 5:35am.

Times had changed since Mario had been born, and he was able to stay beside Maria and watch his son come into the world. He timed Maria's contractions, writing each one down on a piece of paper. He described the experience of seeing his flesh and blood being born as 'terrific and such a joy.' He didn't feel nervous, loving every bit of it, and felt transformed as he held his son for the first time.

Two years after Mario became a first-time father, and two days after he celebrated his thirty-second birthday, on the 5th May, 1983, his own father was at home when he suffered a heart attack. Mario just happened to be visiting at the time with Robbie. Cesario was talking to Mario and Robbie but wasn't making much sense. Mario sensed that something was wrong but before anything could be done, Cesario started doubling over in pain. They acted quickly and called Dr Killerby, the doctor on duty that night. Unfortunately, because it was dark, the doctor couldn't find the house easily. He drove quickly up and down the street, knowing that every second was precious and feeling frustrated because he was wasting time. Finally, he found the house and bounded up the steps, knocking on the door loudly. He was let in and immediately set to work. Mario signed a consent form to allow an ambulance to be called while Dr Killerby checked on Cesario. Once the ambulance arrived, Cesario was taken to the hospital and placed in the Intensive Care Unit. He remained there for about a week, and then was transferred to a normal ward. He didn't make any real improvement, the heart attack having caused too much damage. After a couple of days, in the loving embrace of his wife, Cesario died. His children had the opportunity to say goodbye to their father, but Mario didn't get that last chance to see his Dad, to speak those final sentiments to the man he admired and loved dearly. The family feared Mario wouldn't be able to handle seeing his father slipping away, that his mental health would deteriorate again after such a traumatic event. In trying to protect Mario, he was prevented from spending any final moments next to his father. It was of course done in the best of intentions, however Mario, for the rest of his life was deeply saddened by that lack of closure. He so much wished that he had been able to have a final conversation with the man who raised him and whom he dearly loved. After an initial outpouring of tears and grief, the intense emotions were once more bottled up and stored away. Mario put on a brave face at the funeral and forever afterwards, hiding his upset and crying no more.

As is the way of life, though, people must carry on after losing pieces of themselves, moving forward as best as they can with an ache in their heart, keeping their loved ones alive in their memories and thinking of them always as they go about their day to day life. Mario had a wife and a two-year-old son to support, so he kept working as best as he could, saddened by the fact that his son would have no memory of his Nonno.

The sorrow of death is lessened by the joy of new life and Mario and Maria thought it was time to add to their family of three. Suzanne Marie was born in November, 1984 at 1:35pm. Her birth date was like a reminder of the Nonno she would never meet, as she shared the same birthday as Cesario. The new baby daughter Mario now held in his arms eased the sadness of not having him there to celebrate with.

If life was busy with one child, it became even busier with two, and the pressure to provide financially also increased. Maria stayed at home to look after their children, so it was up to Mario to bring in the income and pay off the bills and mortgage. When Suzanne was in pre-primary, Maria became pregnant again, but suffered a miscarriage when she was three months along. Maria was devastated, and while it also saddened Mario, he didn't feel that they could cope financially if they had a third child, so it didn't hit him as hard when they lost the baby.

TOP: *First-time parents holding their baby boy, Matthew, 31st March, 1981.*

ABOVE: *The grave of Mario's father, Cesario, May, 1983.*

TOP: *Mario and Maria with Suzanne, Christmas, 1984.*
ABOVE: *A nice moment between Mario and Suzanne,*
who is 10 months old, September, 1985.

7

The Darkest Decade

In 1993, Mario left the Bunbury Power Station to work at Muja. This was not by choice; they were making workers redundant so he was forced to find work elsewhere. Muja is a power station in Collie, some sixty kilometres inland from Bunbury, producing electricity for the grid. Mario found everything more modern, but didn't like that as there was no one to teach him how to operate the machinery. He didn't settle and felt out of his depth. After being at the Bunbury station for so long and knowing his job inside and out, the uncertainty of the new job was overwhelming.

His mental illness started to get the better of him again, pushing him to breaking point until the simple act of getting up and going to work became too much. At the same time that he was unwell, his new employers were making employees redundant. This time Mario chose the redundancy, knowing he couldn't cope at work anymore. So in late 1993, when Mario was only forty-two, he said goodbye to his working life. That year was extremely tough, and the strain of Mario's illness was felt by the whole family. Maria was five months pregnant with their third child when Mario had a serious relapse. She had to cope with the exhaustion of looking after Matthew and Suzanne, which only added to the tiredness that comes with being pregnant. On top of that, she was travelling back and forth to visit Mario, who had ended up at Sir Charles Gairdner Hospital again, a nearly two hundred-kilometre drive from their home. After some time, Mario was discharged but was not completely better, and he returned to hospital a few months later. He was still an inpatient at Sir Charles Gairdner when Maria was ready to give birth. Alf made the trip up to Perth to bring him back to his home, so he could be there for the birth. Alf drove a Mini Minor, so the confined space caused Mario to feel extremely anxious and agitated. By the time Alf pulled into the driveway, after a bumpy two hour drive, Mario was so wound up and distressed that he plodded quickly up the outside stairs and through the front door. He threw himself onto the couch without even a hello or a glance in his family's direction.

The next day, Maria went into hospital and was induced in the morning. The contractions began not long after, and she laboured until she brought Stephanie Caitlin into the world in February, 1994 at 4:35pm.

Mario was there in body as Maria laboured and eventually gave birth to Stephanie, but his mind was elsewhere. The medication coursed through his body and stunted his emotions, stopping him from experiencing the joy and wonder that comes with meeting one's child for the first time. Maria was left to manage on her own; Mario was in no condition to be helpful in any way. When Maria went back home, Mario was taken back to Sir Charles Gairdner and remained there for about a month. He missed out on the first month of his baby's life, while Maria had to not only care for a newborn, but her two other children too. The family was struggling and Mario's mental illness affected everybody. They were in the midst of their darkest days, the strain and anguish lasting for the next decade. Over that time, Mario was at his worst and sadly, it created a divide between him and his family. Matthew and Suzanne, too young to understand why he was acting so strangely, separated themselves from him, treating him like a stranger, someone to fear. He was in and out of hospital and there were many days spent at the psychiatric unit, the uninviting place becoming as familiar to them all as if it was a normal way to spend time together.

At one point, when Mario was seriously deluded, he believed he was well and didn't need to take his medication anymore. It was clear he needed to be hospitalised, but he was refusing to go. That night was traumatic for the family. Matthew and Suzanne hid in the bedroom, trembling in fear, listening to their father shouting strange things. Thankfully, Stephanie was too young to understand what was going on and was being looked after by Catena, Maria's mother. The neighbours sat outside on their porch, enjoying the free entertainment, listening to the commotion that was going on and speculating about who could be causing such a disturbance at that time of night. Mario was not the violent type; even when experiencing psychotic episodes he didn't hurt anyone, but his actions frightened his family that night. He hugged Maria tightly, squeezing hard and singing to her, not wanting to let her go. When he finally released her, she rang his brother, Tony, afraid of her husband's behaviour. Tony immediately drove to the house, to find Mario angry and yelling.

He kept saying, 'I'm well now. I don't need to take my medication.'

Tony replied, 'Yes you do, Mario. If you don't take it and calm down, I am going to call the police.'

Mario refused to do either and so Tony did as he promised. When the police arrived, Mario had calmed down enough to willingly let the police escort him to the hospital.

On Stephanie's first birthday, Mario was ill again. It was a cruel reminder that this illness followed him and could ruin times that were supposed to be happy. Mario watched on as Stephanie received presents, feeling like a zombie, sluggish and far-removed from the people he loved most. To his mind, with the thoughts he was having, it was all normal. Which was why he picked up a toy doll that his one-year-old girl had just opened and was delighting over, and threw it across the room. The doll hit the door with a thud and fell to the floor. All noise ceased. The laughter and light-heartedness of the party extinguished. To Mario, it was a completely normal thing to do, and he was oblivious to the shock on his family's faces, and the deafening pressure of the silence that filled the room, settling like a wedge between him and his wife and children.

Years passed, but Mario's illness followed, as did the unspoken hurt within the family. Mario's children grew up but didn't grow closer to him. He was harsh, a strict disciplinarian, unable to relate to his own flesh and blood. No one understood the other, a dysfunctional family trying to function as best as they knew how. Mario no longer worked, so he was a constant presence in the home, his days spent wandering aimlessly around the house, unmotivated and not well enough to do anything. His numerous medications made him tired, so he would sleep a lot during the day. He was trapped in his own personal hell, his mind stopping him from doing things that would be easy for a healthy person.

In 2000, as soon as he turned eighteen, Matthew moved out of home and went to live in Perth. A year later, Suzanne, just seventeen, also shifted to Perth. This was a blessing in a way, as, once Matthew and Suzanne had some distance,

Mario's relationship with them started to improve, finally beginning to forge a connection with his children.

In 2001, when Mario was in hospital again for a minor relapse, he was found to have Type-2 Diabetes, so the doctors put him on tablets to manage it. This unfortunately meant more medication for Mario and another health problem to have to cope with.

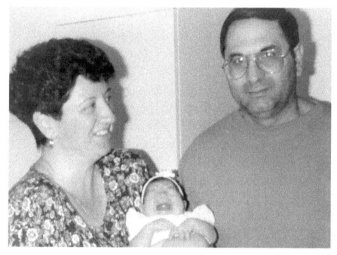

ABOVE: Maria and Mario with baby Stephanie,
St John of God Hospital, 12th February, 1994.

8

Heartache Mixed with Happiness

Matthew, the eldest son, married his teenage sweetheart, Abbey, on the 26th April, 2003. This made Mario extremely happy and proud to see his son marry, but the trip to Perth and the running around the day before the wedding getting last minute details organised was stressful for him. Mario did not travel well, even for short trips to Perth, and what would be no problem for a healthy person was an ordeal for him. Not long after the wedding, in May, Mario felt himself spiralling into another relapse. Once more he had it in his mind that he had been cured and no longer needed his medication. He stopped taking his tablets, and for the next two weeks, he lay in bed, not eating or showering. Nothing Maria could say would convince Mario to take his medication. Desperate, Maria called Lana, a nurse from the hospital who gave Mario his injections. She came to the house, finding Mario in bed. Even she couldn't convince him.

'I hate you!' he shouted at Lana. In response, she called the police. When they arrived, they managed to get him out of bed, into their car and to hospital. All the while, Mario was trying to persuade them that he had been cured.

Mario ended up in the psychiatric unit in Bunbury, staying there for the next sixteen weeks – his longest stay in hospital. He was at his lowest point yet; he wouldn't get out of bed, laying in his own tortured reality for days on end, the nurses unable to get him up and moving. Due to being sedentary for so long, he developed a blood clot in his leg. Maria and the nurse, Andrea, had to massage his legs to keep the blood circulating.

As they did, Andrea said sadly to Maria, 'Mario has really got himself into a hole.' This hole was deep, metaphorically speaking, and it would take everything he had to climb his way out. The journey was long and hard, the power of the mind an unyielding enemy, depression and dark thoughts consuming him and making the days feel like they were never-ending. When his mind was full of thoughts that were not his own, when he became so anxious and restless that he couldn't sit still, he paced. Up and down, back and forth, round and round in circles. Like a caged animal waiting for its chance to escape, he prowled the halls of the hospital, waiting for his mind to let him go free. While the sun rose and fell, Mario remained inside, under artificial light and with only a stark, sanitised clock on the wall to indicate the passing of time. Within these walls he slowly began to return to reality. Days turned into weeks, and as they did, the medication began to reassert itself, reassert his personality. The fog that clouded his mind cleared, and he was able to start participating in things that he enjoyed. There was an older Italian woman on the ward who had suffered a nervous breakdown, their heritage giving them a common link. They would sit at a table, playing Italian cards and passing time together. Thankfully, the ward also had a workshop, which happened to be exactly what Mario needed to bring him back up out of that hole. In this workshop were the tools of his trade, machinery he could pick up and use easily, his hands still able to create and mould something from nothing. He would spend hours doing metalwork and woodwork, and the nurses were impressed with what he crafted from blocks of wood. Bookshelves, cup-stands, chopping boards – all born from a man who had lost his mind on several occasions but found it again, never losing his intellect.

Then finally, after months of rehabilitation, Mario was able to go home. Happy to be back in his own familiar environment, he adjusted quickly, appreciating the simple pleasures of his life: Maria's cooking and company, his own bed and couch, the ability to go visit his brothers and spend time with family.

But as is the way with the see-saw of life, it seems to bring heartache and happiness, teasing one with good times before knocking down these heights of joy and bringing another challenge. The next battle Mario faced, after spending so long combatting his mental health, was the death of his much-loved mother, Maria. She passed away on the 22nd of September, 2004, at the age of ninety-three. At the time of her death, she was living at St. Vincent's, a nursing home that took full-time care of their patients. Maria's body was weak and frail, old age crippling her and taking away her ability to look after herself. Mario used to visit and sit with her weekly, sharing coffee and conversation. He saw her a week before she died and when he kissed her on the cheek, said goodbye and walked out of her room, he had no idea that it would be the final time he saw his mother alive. Mario had actually been suffering another relapse and was assigned once more to the psychiatric unit in the lead up to his mother's death, but it so happened that he was home on a temporary leave. He received a phone call from his youngest brother, Tony, telling him of the news – that she had bled out from her uterus until her limbs went numb and she lost consciousness. The doctor and priest were there, the priest giving her a final blessing before she passed away. Tony had been there too, watching as she took her last breath. Yet again, Mario missed out on the chance for final goodbyes. He didn't waste any time in getting to the nursing home after the call. Tony's daughter, Nicole, also rushed to the nursing home and they both hugged each other, Mario clearly very upset. They went into the room, finding the frail lady tucked up in bed, looking like she was in a peaceful slumber. He walked over to the bed, sat down and placed her hand in his, the warmth of her palm still lingering. Mario was glad to have been able to see his mother one last time but wished she could have heard his farewell. He felt some peace, though, knowing she was now in a better place.

The brutal finality that comes with losing a loved one is the hardest burden to bear, the knowledge that they are gone for good causing an ache that cannot be fixed. Mario had to be careful not to let his grief get the better of him. He had to control his fragile state of mind and couldn't afford to let this consume him. Even at the funeral, when his mother was being lowered into the ground, he kept telling himself, 'I've got to be strong. I've got to be strong.' Mario managed to pull himself together, and continued to focus on becoming well again so he could be discharged from hospital, a place that was very familiar to him but was a stifling reminder of the unwell man that he was.

With his mantra becoming a focus, Mario did indeed manage to become more stable and a few years passed by rather uneventfully. The medications also helped, finally stabilising his Schizophrenia. The doctors had changed the type of drug they were giving him, targeting the chemical imbalance rather than the whole brain. This made Mario feel less sluggish and zombie-like and helped him think clearer. Years of being on various medications had taken their toll, and had weakened Mario's body, making him unable to do much. He would spend his days pottering around the house, thinking of all the jobs that needed doing but feeling completely unmotivated to do any of them. The medication made him tired, so he slept a lot. Days, weeks and years passed by in this way. When Mario felt well, he would visit his brothers. He was always happy to hear how their lives were going even when his own was at a standstill.

In 2007, Mario's daughter, Suzanne, having had enough of living in Perth and wanting to be closer to her family, moved back home. Mario enjoyed having his two daughters under the one roof again. It was only temporary, though, as Suzanne soon became engaged to her boyfriend, so Mario knew she would only be there until she married. He was pleased that she would still remain close by once married, choosing to stay in Bunbury rather than going back to Perth.

His brother, Alf, started to become unwell and then diagnosed with Leukaemia. It didn't take long for this disease to shut down his body, and on the 9th of September, 2008, he passed away in hospital. Mario felt saddened watching his brother weaken, succumbing to the horrible disease that takes away the person and leaves a shell of the man. Not one to show his emotions, Mario kept this sadness inside, knowing all too well by now that death is a part of life. He believed Alf was resting in peace, along with his father and mother, and so again, Mario carried on with life and cherished the family he still had with him. Not long after Alf's death, on the 22nd of November, 2008, Suzanne was married to Jordan, the brother of Abbey, Matthew's wife. Mario considered Jordan as another son and was honoured to be walking his daughter down the aisle, leading her to the man he confidently felt would take great care of his daughter.

ABOVE: Mario stands proudly with Matthew on his wedding day, 26ᵗʰ April, 2003.

ABOVE: Mario getting ready to walk his daughter, Suzanne, down the aisle, 22nd November, 2008.

9

Cancer Comes Calling

Mario became a Nonno for the first time in August, 2009, when Matthew and Abbey welcomed Jesaia Max into the world. A couple of days after the birth, Mario went to Perth with Maria and met his grandson, holding an incredible new life in his arms and feeling very proud and blessed to have another addition to the family.

In 2010, Mario suffered another health set-back, but this time it wasn't related to his Schizophrenia. He had just made himself a cup of tea and was placing it on the table, when his left hand and arm went numb and he lost feeling to the area. He managed to set his tea down, sat down and finished his drink, not feeling any different except for the numb sensation in his hand and arm, which lasted for about five minutes. A couple days later, he went to the doctor for a routine check-up, and mentioned what had happened. After running some tests, it was discovered that Mario had actually suffered a stroke. Amazingly, the CAT scan showed only a small shadow on the back of his brain that had been affected, but not enough for it to impact on his well-being. Having spent years being sick, he'd learnt how to stay positive and remain focused on getting better. This was just another bump in his health troubles and so he kept the smile on his face as he continued on with life.

Two years passed, and then Mario received some more good news – he was going to be a Nonno for the second time, as Abbey was pregnant again.

Two months before the baby was due, Mario went to see the doctor for his usual routine visit and the doctor noticed Mario was pale and looked unwell, so he requested a colonoscopy. Unfortunately, they found that he had bowel cancer. The doctors were able to act quickly, operating and removing the part of his bowel that was affected. His surgery took place on the 14th September, 2012. It was a nervous wait for the family, the surgery taking a couple of hours to complete. He took a long time coming out of the anaesthetic, the drugs causing him to stay in a deep slumber for longer than normal. This was obviously good for Mario's recuperation but the rest of the patients on the ward must not have thought so as his snoring was like a train rumbling through the ward. It was really, really loud, so much so that almost out of embarrassment the nurses, Maria and Suzanne called into his ear to waken him. Once he was awake, Mario was sore but in high spirits, and this attitude helped him bounce back from the surgery quickly. The doctors considered the operation a success and decided that he didn't need chemotherapy. This was such a relief for all the family and they put this incident to the back of their minds, thankful for the positive outcome and happy to move forward as Mario went back to his old self and the family kept going with their busy lives. Abbey duly gave birth to grandchild number two, Coby Cruz, in November, 2012 and Mario was again filled with pride and love.

Another two years went by and as they did the feelings of fear that had come with that first diagnosis of cancer were eased. Little did any of the family know that it was only a matter of time before they would have to face this fear again. Sadly, the hurdles and obstacles were not going to be as easy to overcome the second time around.

TOP LEFT: *Mario meets his first grandson, Jesaia, for the first time, September, 2009.*

TOP RIGHT: *Three generations, September, 2009.*

ABOVE: *Mario happily holding his second grandson, Coby, 2013.*

10

Diagnosed with Secondary Liver Cancer

Mario was overjoyed to learn that Suzanne was pregnant. He found out in March 2014, and enjoyed watching the pregnancy develop over the next nine months. In December, 2014, Emmy Isabella was born. As mother and baby were settled into the maternity ward, Mario gazed down at his first granddaughter. The smile on his face and the deep-seated joy reflected in his eyes spoke of the instant love he felt for this newest little one. He was radiant with happiness and that was only to be added to a few weeks later when Matthew, Abbey, Jesaia and Coby moved from Perth to Bunbury to live.

Life was good. He finally had all his children and grandchildren in the same town. He hadn't had a relapse in a very long time, and he had a happy attitude despite all his past hurdles. He loved watching Emmy grow and develop, from a tiny newborn into a healthy and happy baby. Then, a month before Emmy's first birthday, Mario began to feel sick. Unaware that what he was experiencing was the start of a serious health problem, one that wouldn't be easily fixed. It started a couple of weeks after Maria returned from a four-week trip to Italy. Three generations of the family – mum, Catena, sister, Gina, and daughter, Stephanie, had accompanied Maria back to visit the old country. Mario didn't want to go, mostly due to his many health problems; it would have been very difficult for him to sit on the plane for so long, and then walk around sightseeing. His body wasn't cut out for travelling, but he was happy to know that Maria was finally going back to see her country of birth, even though Mario had never returned to visit the place where it all began for him. He missed Maria, having never been away from her for so long without being able to see her, but the time passed by quickly. He would have dinner with Suzanne, Jordan and Emmy three to four nights a week, and received dinner invites for the other nights too. Not wishing to spend the evenings alone, he found that this arrangement worked well for him. Because Emmy saw a lot of him throughout those four weeks, she started to develop a closer bond with her Nonno, and since that time had an obvious and expressive love for him, even saying 'Nonno' as one of her first words.

Mario had a colonoscopy booked for the 18th of November, 2015. This was simple routine given he had bowel cancer previously. A few nights before the procedure, he started having strong stomach pains, with episodes of diarrhoea and then constipation. He put it down to maybe having a virus.

The preparation and colonoscopy went smoothly, but afterwards, Mario started to develop severe back pain. He complained to the now returned Maria about it, and she thought that it might have been a result of his colonoscopy, that maybe they had hurt his back while trying to move him on the table, as he was a rather heavy man. But the pain continued and so Maria took him to the Emergency Department at the hospital on the 25th November. After running some tests, the doctors found that he had two clots in his liver. One of these clots was in the portal vein, the main artery to the liver. He was taken to the Intensive Care Unit and closely monitored overnight, and the next day, they moved him to the surgical ward at the Bunbury Regional Hospital, putting him on a liquid diet in case they needed to take him to surgery. He remained in hospital for a week, the doctors putting him on Warfarin, a drug used to thin the blood so the clots could dissolve. The tests that were taken when Mario first went to hospital showed that a large portion of the liver was damaged and that the spleen was beyond repair. The doctors didn't seem concerned about the spleen, though – it was the liver that needed attention. After running more scans, the doctors informed Maria and Mario that they had seen some lesions on his liver, and so a biopsy was booked. This procedure took place on the 30th November, a simple and routine technique that meant they only needed to numb the area. Mario was able to watch as they inserted the long needle into his stomach. He felt fine afterwards, although the pain was still present, coming and going, but not as severe as he had experienced before. He was discharged on the 2nd of December, 2015, very relieved to be home and resting in a familiar, comfortable place. Suzanne was especially relieved, as it was Emmy's first birthday party in a couple of days and Suzanne wanted him to be there for his granddaughter's first birthday. Unfortunately, though, a blood test that Mario had undergone showed a very low blood count, suggesting that he had an internal bleed somewhere. The doctor rang their home first thing on the morning of Emmy's birthday and told Maria to get Mario to the Emergency Department as soon as possible. Both fretted that they were to miss their granddaughter's special first birthday, but the worry everyone felt for Mario was more pressing. The spectre of cancer loomed in everyone's mind.

The harsh reality was confirmed on the 7th of December. Mario was still in hospital and had been told the doctor would come that morning to give him the results of the biopsy. Maria and Suzanne anxiously waited with Mario, passing the time by trying to keep Emmy entertained on a hospital bed. Minutes turned to hours, then finally, just before lunch, the doctor walked in. Despite his training, the man's expression couldn't hide that he was the bearer of bad news. The curtain was closed for privacy, but the other patients could still hear, no doubt feeling awkward that they were privy to the moment a family was made aware that their lives would never be the same again.

The doctor explained that the lesion was cancerous, a secondary cancer that was most likely due to the bowel cancer he had years ago. Mario just sat there, smiling at the doctor. He appeared calm and collected, not acting like a man who had just been told that he had cancer for a second time. Being hard of hearing shielded Mario from the news, but Maria and Suzanne heard every word, hearts sinking as the ephemeral thoughts of *maybe it's cancer* became hardened into the permanent truth – *it's definitely cancer.*

The doctor didn't stay long. No doubt many instances of being the messenger ensured that he simply said his piece and then withdrew. There hadn't been much discussion. Maria and Suzanne were too stunned to form any coherent questions. Emmy was fidgeting and getting grizzly, as if she could sense that something wasn't quite right. All that Maria and Suzanne took away from the conversation was that the cancer was back, not in the bowel but in the liver, that it wasn't going to be as straightforward as an operation this time, chemotherapy would be needed, and they should wait for a phone call from the oncologist to set up an appointment time. When the doctor left, Mario looked at Maria and Suzanne, still smiling while they tried to hold back tears.

'What did the doctor say, Darling?' Mario asked, confirming that he didn't take from the conversation what Maria and Suzanne had. Trying to talk as softly as possible, aware that there were other patients in the room still listening to this difficult exchange, Maria said, 'You have liver cancer. You will need chemotherapy but we have to wait to see the oncologist.'

A pause. A moment for Mario to take in the information and process it. And then a response, 'Oh…well I've beaten this once; I'll have to do it again.'

A couple days after that, Mario was discharged from hospital and all they could do now was wait for the appointment that would give them more information and tell them where to go from here. It was more of an anxious wait for the family, Mario seemingly unaffected, or maybe unable to grasp the seriousness of the situation. The phone call finally came, and an appointment was made for the 18th of December at 9:50am.

When this day came, only a week and a half after finding out the bad news, yet feeling to the family like a lifetime, Mario walked into the oncology clinic with his support crew – Maria, Matthew, Suzanne and Stephanie. The oncologist was a lady whose immediate bedside manner could have been warmer. She wasn't exactly welcoming when she saw the five of them enter the room, seemingly put out by the fact that she had to get some extra chairs for them. When all were settled, she asked Mario what symptoms he had been experiencing and he explained what had been happening to him – the stomach and back pain, the constant trips to the toilet, sometimes having diarrhoea, the other times constipation, which only made the pain worse. She scribbled notes on a piece of paper, all the while knowing what was causing these symptoms. She then reiterated what the doctor had said in the hospital: that the lesions on Mario's liver were metastatic cancer, most likely originating from the bowel cancer he had three years earlier; that he would require chemotherapy; that he also had lymph nodes in his stomach that appeared cancerous. This last piece of information was new, though, and made any hope of a positive outcome seem more unlikely. To be sure about the state of the lymph nodes, they would have to do a PET scan; this would also determine if the cancer had spread anywhere else. Mario appeared to be off in his own world, not taking much in and not really understanding much of what was being said.

Suzanne and Matthew had come prepared with questions, and took turns asking them.

'What stage is the cancer?'

Another shock rocked the family as the doctor answered, 'It's stage four.'

'How many stages are there?'

'Four.'

Their hearts sank. That single word hung in the air, before falling like a leaden weight, making an impact and crushing any hope. Its echoes filled the room with a long drawn out silence. Then the doctor looked at Mario and asked a question herself.

'Do you want to know the outlook for this type of cancer?'

Mario said yes, and she calmly went on to say that without treatment, it could be twelve months, and with treatment, maybe up to twenty-four months. This all started to feel very real for Maria and the children, but Mario still seemed unaffected, the harsh truth going over his head. The rest of the appointment was spent talking about the chemotherapy and explaining the options Mario had to receive this treatment. He could either have a pump that he would take home and have connected to him for a couple of days, or he could have it injected into him, which would take about three hours in the oncology clinic at the hospital. He chose the latter, and an appointment was made to start on the 23rd of December.

While standing with Suzanne, waiting for Maria to finish making the appointment, he said, 'I hope I survive this.'

It was this statement, and others that he would make over the next couple of weeks, that made Suzanne and the rest of the family think that he was still oblivious to what the doctor had told them. This wouldn't be like the last time; surgery wouldn't remove the cancer, and there was no second chance. It was simply a matter of how long. Not if, but when.

After going home and thinking about it, Mario decided to postpone his appointment, with Christmas being only two days after his treatment. He didn't want to be feeling sick with side effects, he wanted to enjoy Christmas with his family, and so Maria called and changed the appointment. The family thought it was best to hold off telling Mario the prognosis and wait until after the festivities, letting him enjoy the day. Then, after more thought, they decided to not say anything at all, not wanting to risk Mario giving up hope. He had been so positive throughout all of it so far, and the family wanted to make sure he kept a positive frame of mind, because they knew he couldn't afford to go back down the dark road of depression and despair.

Mario enjoyed Christmas with his family, not looking or feeling the best but making the most of the day. Five days later, on the 30th of December, Mario had his first chemotherapy treatment. The nurse checked his blood pressure first, and when she saw it was through the roof she joked, 'Whoa, do you think I'm nice, Mario?'

They all had a laugh, easing the tension that the family was obviously feeling, and the next time she checked his blood pressure, it had returned to normal. Maria and Suzanne sat with him the whole time, Mario appreciating the company as it helped the time pass a little quicker. It was a long session, taking about three hours to complete. Mario dealt with it very well, managing to sit for the duration without getting fidgety. He even exclaimed at one point, 'I am a champion!'

But then the time came for the nurses to flush the drugs through his system, the pump starting off slowly and then ticking louder as it coursed faster through the vein in his hand. The feeling became unpleasant and made Mario anxious for it to finish. Squirming in the chair, he said to Maria, 'Darling, get the nurses, turn it off.'

Suzanne encouraged him, saying, 'You've come this far, not long now, you can do it.'

This helped calm him down and got him through the rest. 'Thanks, I needed to hear that.'

The thanks was not lost on Suzanne. It's not just children who need moral support; as the world turns and the years pass, parents need borrowed strength when theirs is dwindling. When the session was over, they walked back to the car, Mario with shaky legs and a pale face, and Maria and Suzanne looking at him and thinking the battle had well and truly begun now.

Once home, Mario began to feel nauseous and restless, pacing around the lounge like a caged animal. The powerful drugs coursed through his body, an unseen force raging beneath his skin. He went to the bathroom, his unsettled stomach causing him to heave, but with no result. He came out, but then went back to the bathroom, this time bringing up a bit of liquid. Maria's mother and sister came around to see how he was, and Stephanie and Suzanne were there as well. It was soon evident that this was what Mario needed most. His family and friends around him, surrounded by the people he loved. He began to feel better, and surprisingly, after that, he had no more nausea, bouncing back and making the family hope that he might actually handle chemotherapy better than expected.

On the 4th of January, Mario had his PET scan. Then more than a week of waiting, filled with worrying and wondering if there would be more bad news. On the 15th of January, 2016, after a long week and a half, Mario went to the oncologist with Maria and Suzanne to get more answers. The oncologist didn't say much about the scan at first, talking instead about putting Mario on an additional drug, called Cetuximab, and explaining that this would be a weekly infusion on top of his normal chemotherapy. This meant he would now be going to the hospital each week for the infusion, then every third week for his chemotherapy and infusion. At home he had chemotherapy tablets to take for two weeks, then have a week off. The cycle would then begin again. When asked about the results of the scan, the doctor didn't indicate that the cancer had spread anywhere else. Suzanne asked if the lymph nodes in the stomach were cancerous and the doctor replied that they were, and corrected Suzanne, saying they were in the abdomen, not the stomach.

Suzanne then asked, 'How many are there in the *abdomen?*'

To which the doctor responded by simply saying, 'Lots.'

A couple of days after that appointment, Mario noticed blood in his urine. He didn't say anything to Maria at first, thinking it might be a one-off, not wanting to cause alarm again. But the next day, the blood was still there so he told Maria. Back to the Emergency Department they went, both becoming very familiar with the place after the last couple of months. Scans were done, but nothing showed up. The doctor said it could possibly be an infection, so he prescribed Mario some antibiotics and told him that he would need to see a urologist to investigate it further.

Two days later, on the 21st of January, Mario had his long session at the hospital, having his normal chemotherapy, then the Cetuximab. Mario went to the hospital in pain – that morning he had woken up with a sharp pain in his stomach.

When the nurse was connecting him up to the machine, he felt nauseous. The nurse gave him a vomit bag and some Panadol, and thankfully the pain subsided, making the session easier to get through. As always, Maria was by his side the whole time, and Suzanne and Emmy came and spent some time with him, too. Mario felt he could get through anything when his family was around him, and he finished another round of chemotherapy with a smile on his face. Fortunately, he tolerated the treatment well and didn't have any major side effects. His family was expecting the chemotherapy to knock Mario around, especially when he had the additional drug. But Mario surprised everyone, his fighting spirit evident to those around him.

The next week went by without any problems, until the day that Mario and Maria had to face yet another hurdle – this time involving a crucial piece of information that was first discovered years ago and should have been passed throughout the entire family.

TOP: Mario lovingly holds his first granddaughter, Emmy, 2015.

ABOVE: Some snapshots of Mario enjoying Christmas with his family, December, 2015.

ABOVE: Mario's joy captured after receiving a framed collage of various photos from his youth, Christmas, December, 2015.

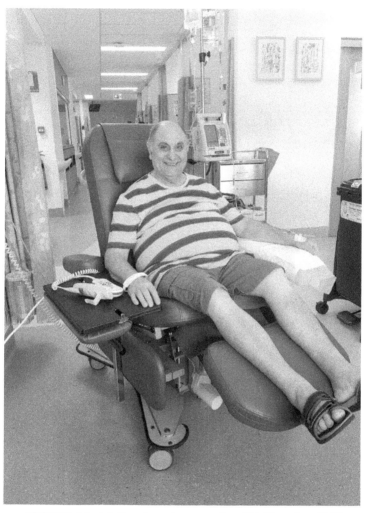

ABOVE: Mario's first chemotherapy session, 30ᵗʰ December, 2015.

11

A Family Discovery and a Near Death Experience

During a conversation with a family member, Maria found out that in 2013, a cancer gene had been discovered in the Spinelli family. With this being the case, Mario needed to get tested. If he carried this mutated gene, then his children would also need to be tested. This was the first Maria had heard of it.

Maria passed on this information to Mario, Matthew, Suzanne and Stephanie, knowing that it would cause stress but realising that they needed to know. Matthew didn't show much interest in getting tested as he felt that there was no point – if he was found to be positive, it would cause anxiety over something that couldn't be controlled. But Suzanne and Stephanie were keen to be tested; being female put them at a higher risk of developing cancer if they were positive. Maria started making enquiries with their doctor to see if she could get a referral for Mario to be tested.

Mario saw the urologist on the 9th of February, 2016. He was told the same thing as previously – that the blood in his urine may have been due to an infection, and as the antibiotics seemed to have cleared it up, he didn't seem too concerned. The specialist booked Mario in for a procedure anyway, just to be sure. He couldn't get in until March 15th, which meant, as usual, having to wait to find out more answers. After visiting the urologist, Mario went to dinner with his family, celebrating Stephanie's 22nd birthday. He was in his element, always appreciating the time he got to spend with those he loved. He enjoyed his meal that night, and polished his plate clean. Since he had started having stomach pains he didn't enjoy food like he used to, his appetite diminishing dramatically. So things were looking up for him to be able to eat well.

Maybe the chemotherapy was helping. Maybe there was hope. But if there had been a crystal ball sitting at the table that night, if the family had looked into it to see what was coming, they would have talked to Mario a little more, enjoyed his company and conversation a little longer, appreciated his presence and hugged him a little tighter.

A few days later, Mario was due for his third round of chemotherapy, but when he had the routine blood test the day before, he was found to have low platelets, which means chemotherapy could not be given. He went in for his Cetuximab infusion, which only took an hour. He went home early, unaware that the next few days of semi-normalcy were about to come crashing down. Mario was about to undertake his biggest fight yet, a challenge that would alter the path of his already limited future.

On Monday the 15th of February, Mario woke early, looking forward to the day. Maria and Mario were going to Jordan and Suzanne's house to look after Emmy, while they went to Perth for an appointment. Mario, as always, embraced Jordan and Suzanne, and gave Emmy a kiss in greeting. He would always hug them hello and goodbye, even if he had seen them the day before, his face always lighting up with a big smile, as if he hadn't seen them in ages. As Suzanne finished getting ready, Mario and Jordan spoke about everyday things, Mario commenting about Jordan's green lawn and Jordan asking how the clearing out of Mario's shed was going. When it was time to go, Mario stood at the door and waved goodbye to Jordan and Suzanne, saying, 'Have a good day. See you tonight.'

They had planned to stay for dinner that night, but as the morning went on, it was clear that those plans would be abandoned. The family dinner never eventuated; instead it was replaced with an event that would terrify them all.

An hour or so after Jordan and Suzanne left, Mario began to feel sleepy. He lay down on the couch, but wasn't there for long, unable to actually sleep. He got up and went to where Maria was playing with Emmy. He complained to Maria that he had a headache, and when Maria turned to look at him, she noticed that the left side of his face looked a little droopy. She thought it may have been caused from the way he had been laying on the couch, so didn't give it another thought. Mario was quiet after that, his headache bothering him enough to not interact with Emmy as much as he normally would. Lunchtime came, and Maria put a sandwich on the table for Mario.

Not long after Mario said, 'Darling, my hand has gone numb.'

Maria looked across the table, and food was falling from Mario's mouth and onto the floor. Immediately, alarm bells went off in her head as she remembered the symptoms of his last stroke. Trying not to panic, Maria quickly called her sister, Gina, and explained what was happening. Luckily, Gina was only a suburb away, so she swung around and was at the house within fifteen minutes. Mario was calmly walking around and laughed when Gina walked in the door.

'Mario,' she said, 'Best you get yourself to hospital.'

Maria left Emmy with Gina, and drove Mario to the Emergency Department. It was busy, so they were told to wait, but when Mario started to slur his speech they were seen immediately. At first, another stroke was suspected, and the doctor organised a scan of the head. While they were waiting for the results, Mario needed the toilet urgently. They couldn't allow him to go, having to closely monitor him, so the doctor gave him a container, closed the curtain and left him to it. His hand went numb again while holding the container and Mario lost his grip on the handle, dropping the container and spilling urine all over the floor and onto Maria's handbag. Mario knew this wasn't his fault, but was still embarrassed. This lack of control was only just the beginning. Mario's dignity was being diminished, along with the man everyone knew.

It was clear Mario was not going home that night – the scan revealed that he had suffered a bleed on the right side of his brain. The doctors believed it was caused by the injections he was taking daily, blood thinners that helped control the clots in his liver. He was admitted to hospital and closely monitored by the nursing staff. The doctors told Maria that they would call her if there was any change so she said goodbye and told Mario she would be back in the morning. At the point that Maria left him to go home, he was still able to talk and use his left arm. The periods of slurred speech and the numb hand were intermittent and didn't last long. Mario tried to sleep that night, but the hourly visits from the nurses to check his vital signs kept disturbing him.

Morning came, the new day bringing not hope, but the beginning of a long nightmare. By the time Suzanne came to visit him, Mario had begun to slur his speech again, this time being very difficult to understand, and had lost the use of his left arm. He watched Suzanne's shocked expression and her inability to remain composed, as she struggled to understand what he was trying to say. He watched her face crumple and the tears roll down her cheeks. She turned away from him so she could gather herself, trying to pull it together so she could be strong for him. His mind worked hard to form the words that would have normally come easily to him.

'Don't cry,' he said, managing to make that understood.

The doctor came and introduced himself to Suzanne, saying that Mario had begun to deteriorate that morning, and a second scan showed the bleed had become bigger. The night before, the doctors thought it would be best to keep him in Bunbury, but now that his condition had deteriorated, they made the decision to transfer him to Sir Charles Gairdner Hospital in Perth, as soon as possible. Suzanne phoned Maria, desperately hoping that she was on her way. Maria was at home getting ready to go back to the hospital as she hadn't heard from the hospital overnight, and she assumed nothing had changed. After Suzanne explained what was happening, she hung up and rushed over, and when she saw Mario and the condition he was in, she was as shocked as Suzanne had been. Mario could only watch on helplessly as his wife and daughter tried to come to terms with what they were witnessing. Maria was angry that the hospital hadn't phoned to let her know, but the doctor explained that this had all happened that morning.

Then the bedlam began. The doctors organised the transport: Mario would be picked up in an ambulance and taken to the Bunbury airport, where the Royal Flying Doctor Service would be ready and waiting to fly him up to Perth. Maria and Suzanne made phone calls, frantic and hurried, the disbelief of what was transpiring gripping them. Over the next hour or two, the family came together, drawn to one another for support and comfort, wishing to visit Mario's bedside, unsure and uncertain if these were to be his last moments. Stephanie, Matthew, Gina, Catena and others floated in and out – Andrea, Frank, Antoinette, Robbie, Angie, Abbey with Jesaia and Coby, Struan, Jordan with Emmy. Even though Mario was incapable of speaking, he understood and recognised everyone. He was a prisoner in his own body, with a fear that he was unable to express. At 1:30pm, the ambulance officers came through the door with a stretcher, and the family had to wait as the curtains were closed and Mario was shifted. When Mario had been moved onto the bed and the curtains opened, the family gathered around him again, offering words of encouragement and saying goodbye. Like a procession, they followed the ambulance officers as they wheeled Mario out into the oppressive Australian heat, where the ambulance was waiting. Anxiety mixed with the humidity enveloped them, the urgency of the situation pressing down on them. They saw it on the faces of the ambulance officers, but they took the time to say their goodbyes again, because, at this point, anything could happen. Mario's life thread was very fragile. They watched as he was placed into the back of the ambulance, then the doors closed and the van drove off. While Mario was being driven to the airport, and then flown to Sir Charles Gairdner, his family was preparing to drive up to Perth. By the time Maria, Matthew, Suzanne and Stephanie arrived at Sir Charles Gairdner and found the ward where Mario had been taken, he had already been set up in the High Dependency Unit on the Neurological ward. Relief flooded Mario when he saw his family by his bedside, but he was so sleepy and couldn't make himself understood. Tubes came out of everywhere; a catheter had been put in, along with an oxygen mask, which Mario kept trying to remove. He was clearly uncomfortable, agitated and restless, his immobile arm and leg limp by his side while his other hand and leg moved constantly, as if fighting an unseen attacker, but it was a losing battle. He was taken away for another scan of the head, which thankfully revealed that the bleed wasn't any bigger. The doctors spoke to Maria, Matthew and Stephanie, explaining that, because the bleed hadn't worsened, they would just monitor Mario frequently throughout the night and see how he went. They believed surgery wasn't an option at that time because it would be too risky, the chance of Mario making it out of the operation too slim. They spoke about the possibility of waiting a couple of weeks, so the blood could unclot, and then operating. This was a less invasive procedure that would just require keyhole surgery. They called this type of surgery Burr holes, a small hole being drilled into the skull, allowing blood to drain, thus relieving pressure on the brain. The thought of keeping Mario in the state he was in for two weeks was unthinkable. He may not even make it that long. But no more could be done that night, and there wasn't much the family could do. So they left him in the hands of the doctors and nurses and went to a nearby hotel, where they would suffer a night of restless, broken sleep, waiting on edge for a phone call to deliver more bad news.

Morning came, Mario having spent the night flitting in and out of sleep, trapped in a nightmare that didn't disappear whenever he woke. His family returned, finding him as they left him, thankful that he was at least still alive. Then the seizures started. This was common with brain haemorrhages, the pressure on the brain causing stress. Mario could feel them coming, powerless to control or stop the convulsions. His left hand would seize up, twitching uncontrollably, and his head did the same thing. The nurses stood by and watched; all they could do was time how long each seizure lasted. It was very distressing for Mario's family to stand by and watch helplessly as his body reacted to the trauma going on inside his brain. They could only imagine how distressing it was for Mario, who would have undoubtedly felt alone and scared. He had just suffered another seizure when Gina, Catena and Andrea arrived, support for Maria, Matthew, Suzanne and Stephanie at a much needed time. Visitors were restricted to two at a time, so they took turns being by Mario's side.

While this was going on, the family also had to worry about what this would mean for getting Mario tested for the BRCA1 gene. Mario and Maria had been in the process of getting a referral from the doctor to see a genetic counsellor and make an appointment to have his blood tested. They had been told that Mario needed to be tested first, as that would determine whether his children would need to also have blood taken for analysis. Then the haemorrhage had happened, and suddenly it felt like time was running out. Suzanne asked a nurse whether it would be possible to get some blood taken from Mario, and sent to the genetic services at King Edward Memorial Hospital. The nurse replied that she would need to pass on the message, not being able to help directly. When it was clear that the question had been forgotten, Suzanne called the genetic clinic directly. The phone rang out, going to an answering machine. Suzanne tried very hard to condense the events of the last couple of days, explaining the urgency with which they now faced, and asked for someone to call her back. All that could be done now was wait and hope for the phone call that would hopefully sort out one problem.

Medication was given to try and stop the seizures, but as the day wore on they became more frequent. The doctors planned to call Mario's oncologist, to discuss his current situation and his cancer prognosis, and then determine whether it was worth operating or not. They had to decide what was the best option, weighing up the benefits and risks of each possible scenario. They were extremely cautious about operating, feeling that the major risk would be a great loss of blood, which could have fatal consequences. His blood was so thin due to the anticoagulant medication he had been on, and this made the decision to operate difficult. The doctors didn't inform Maria about the result of their conversation with his oncologist, but when Mario had a seizure that lasted for over ten minutes, a decision had to be made quickly. Gina, Catena and Andrea had only recently left to drive back home to Bunbury. It happened at about 6:00pm, when Maria, Matthew, Suzanne and Stephanie were there. He felt it coming on, and managed to warn Maria.

'Here comes another one.'

Maria told the nurses, and they observed him. Minutes passed, and Mario was still twitching. A few more minutes went by with no improvement. Mario's family tried to encourage him, telling him it was going to be okay. The length of the seizure was beginning to take its toll on Mario, who had begun to take short, frantic breaths. The nurses worked around him, picking up their pace as the situation intensified.

One of the nurses said, 'It's time to call Code,' as another nurse told the family they needed to wait outside, ushering them away so the medical staff could do what they needed to do.

A nurse calmly stated, 'Code Blue. Code Blue, Ward G54.'

Maria, Matthew, Suzanne and Stephanie stood outside the entrance to the waiting room. They heard the emergency announcement being broadcast across the ward and it filled them with dread. Huddled together, shocked and frightened, the possibility of losing Mario became a real and immediate threat. As Mario lay fighting an internal battle, the nurses fought for him externally, doing all they could to stop the seizure.

A cleaner saw their despair and went over to them.

'Pray to God, pray to God, it will be okay.' He ushered them inside the waiting room. 'Take a seat and pray to God.'

They sat, and the cleaner left, and all they could do was wait to hear of the outcome. Finally, a nurse came and delivered the news they were hoping to hear – Mario was alive. They went to see him, overwhelmed by relief. But he was not in a good way. Moaning and agitated, he was clearly distressed. The neurosurgeon came, taking the family back into the waiting room to tell them what was happening. This wasn't an easy conversation; the surgeon being clear about the trouble Mario was in. It was evident that the seizures were getting worse and the medication was no longer able to control them. Mario was deteriorating before their very eyes and it was obvious that they would have to act quickly, the option of waiting for the clot to dissolve no longer a possibility. But the options the surgeon presented to Mario's family seemed doomed – to leave him like he was, with the blood in his brain, would mean he would surely die, easily apparent by how much he had already worsened in the space of a day. The other option, to cut his head open and remove the bleed, had serious consequences. This surgery is called a Craniotomy, which involves opening a large part of the skull to allow the clot to be removed. The surgeon still thought it was an extremely risky procedure and one that would be too much for his weak body to handle. There were a number of factors – his clots in his liver, his cancer, his fragile state and coping with being under anaesthetic. But the biggest worry was that he would bleed, and they wouldn't be able to stop it. He would simply bleed to death, on the operating table. And then there was the possibility that if he made it through the operation, they couldn't guarantee if there would be permanent brain damage, meaning Mario could wake up disabled. He would possibly need therapy for the rest of his life, which was limited, considering his cancer diagnosis. On hearing this, Maria couldn't hold back the tears any longer.

'Mario wouldn't want to be disabled. One thing I do know is that he wouldn't want to be disabled.'

The surgeon was gentle and spoke like he understood the difficulty of the decision that lay cruelly before them. Mario was unable to communicate what he wanted, so his family had to make a decision for him. These difficult conversations hadn't really taken place yet with Mario – they thought they had more time than this. The family had assumed they would see Mario's health declining as the cancer slowly took hold of him, and know when it was time to find out what he wanted when it was clear his life was near its end. Never did this urgency to make decisions cross their minds. What did cross their minds was the immense unfairness of it all – that even if he did pull through this operation, he would need to undertake therapy, going through rehabilitation to learn to do things that came easily before. Only to be knocked down permanently by his cancer. All that had happened put chemotherapy on hold indefinitely, giving the cancer a chance to keep spreading throughout his body, shortening his prognosis even further. Life had been cruel when it came to Mario's health, and this was just another battle that he would have to face.

The surgeon suggested that they stay at the hospital, as anything could happen. He told them that he would be back in a couple of hours, to hear what they had decided. The surgeon left them then, the weight of the choice before them heavy and horrid. Not long after, Gina called to say they were home. Maria burst into tears again, telling Gina what had happened since they left the hospital. It was a quick conversation, Gina aware that Maria had to get back to Mario. The next couple of hours were spent off and on by Mario's bed-side, his suffering continuing. He was clearly getting worse, his distress and agitation were increasing by the minute.

The family left him while they went to sit in the waiting room to discuss Mario's fate. The discussion went round in circles, either option seemingly hopeless. If they chose surgery, he might not make it. If they chose to wait, he would most definitely deteriorate until it was too late to do anything. If they chose surgery and he did make it, he might wake up disabled in some way. If he made it, he had a long road to recovery, and even if he recovered enough to go back to semi-normalcy, the cancer would eat away at him, cruelly ending his life. There were a lot of *ifs*, everything uncertain, nothing guaranteed. But it felt cruel to leave him to suffer as he was. Mario was a fighter, and if they could give him a chance to keep fighting, however slim the chances were and however dire the situation seemed, at least they were doing something.

The surgeon came back around 10:30pm, bringing with him the decision that they were going to operate anyway. This brought relief to Mario's family, because even though they were leaning towards this decision, they hadn't completely come to a resolution. They were happy to let the surgeon make the final call, and once that call was made, it took some pressure off them. The surgeon left to start making preparations and not long after, Gina, Catena, Andrea and Frank walked through the door. Maria, Matthew, Stephanie and Suzanne all looked up, not expecting to see them at all, their eyes widening and their mouths dropping. They had only made the trip home to Bunbury hours earlier, and now they were back, having driven the almost 200 kilometres up to Perth again, to support the family through this incredibly difficult time. This was one of the reasons Mario loved his family so much; they were always there for each other, ready to help out whenever help was needed. After hugging and thanking them, and wiping away tears of gratitude, Maria, Matthew, Stephanie and Suzanne went to sit by Mario's bedside, spending time with him before the nurses took him away. Mario's condition cemented their decision to operate. He was tormented, pleading with them, 'Please help me!' as he writhed around the bed. Over the course of the few days, when Mario was at his worst, he tried to express his anguish and state of mind. He fought to form the words and make himself understood, each word an effort to speak. Statements such as, 'I want to go home,' 'I can't stand it anymore,' 'I'm like a baby,' 'I'm sorry,' 'I'm not the man I was,' 'I'm embarrassed,' escaped from his lips, breaking the hearts of his family, who were powerless to help.

For all that Mario's family knew, these could be his final hours, and this knowledge sat heavily on their hearts. The nurses began to work around him, doing what they needed to do to get him ready for surgery. The orderly who would wheel the bed to the operating theatre was on his way. The family gathered around Mario's bed, saying their goodbyes. Suzanne asked Matthew to pray the Lord's Prayer, and, as their hands rested on Mario, they began to pray:

'Our Father, Who art in heaven
Hallowed be Thy Name;
Thy kingdom come,
Thy will be done,
on earth as it is in heaven.
Give us this day our daily bread,
and forgive us our trespasses,
as we forgive those who trespass against us;
and lead us not into temptation,
but deliver us from evil. Amen.'

While they were praying, the nurse continued to prepare Mario for surgery, disconnecting and connecting various tubes, a silent witness to this family's desperation. She remained straight-faced, working as if they weren't there, an unintentional intruder to a family's most private moments. The orderly arrived and Mario was wheeled out of the High Dependency Unit and down the corridor to the lifts. The family walked beside the bed, trying to take in these moments, unsure if this would be the last time they saw him alive. Mario was oblivious to what was going on, completely unaware that he was about to undergo massive brain surgery. Time was critical so they couldn't have long goodbyes. They called to him as the elevator opened.

'Good luck.'

'I love you.'

'Keep fighting.'

Mario was wheeled inside and then the doors closed, swallowing Mario and taking him away from their view, and possibly out of their lives for good.

ABOVE: Mario enjoying dinner with family, only a week before his brain bleed, 9ᵗʰ February, 2016.

12

Surviving Brain Surgery

As one day merged unheeded into the next, the clock ticking past midnight and bringing in the 18th February, Mario was wheeled into a theatre room and put under anaesthetic. In the very early hours of the morning, Mario had his head sliced open, exposing his brain and the blood that caused all this horror in the first place. The surgeons worked on Mario for about three hours and stunningly, Mario made it through the surgery with no major complications. He had had a bleed whilst on the table, but the skilled surgeon was able to control it. That had been the major risk – that Mario would bleed out – but thankfully the scenario ended well. When daylight was breaking, Maria received the phone call to say Mario had made it, and their hope, like the sun, rose bright and new. They got to the hospital as soon as they could, having spent a few hours back at the hotel trying to get some rest. They found Mario back in the High Dependency Unit, propped up on pillows, with a feeding tube in his mouth and an oxygen tube up his nose to help him breathe. His mouth drooped, and his left arm still lay lifeless by his side. He struggled to keep his eyes open, trying hard to focus on his family now standing by his bed. His bloodshot eyes rolled around as he moaned and tried to communicate with them. Mario's right hand reached up, trying to scratch at the new wound that snaked across the side of his head. He had an impressive cut that started at his right ear and curved around to the top of his head. His hair, which he didn't have much of in the first place, had been shaved, now bald except for the back and left side of his head. The family didn't know what to expect when they saw him, but it was a shock to find him still so distressed and agitated. The surgeon who had operated on Mario was not there, no doubt home getting some much needed rest, after spending the night saving Mario's life. The nurses informed the family that even though the surgery went well, Mario was continuing to experience seizures, his brain still under a lot of trauma. The road to recovery was long and he was in no way out of danger yet. The team of nurses and doctors were now focusing on controlling the seizures. As the day progressed, the seizures became less in frequency and duration. The next few days would be a game of wait and see, the family only able to take one day at a time, knowing how quickly circumstances can change.

The nurses tried to lighten the mood, many of them commenting on Mario's extremely long eyelashes, joking that women would kill for long eyelashes like his. It was true, Mario did have lengthy lashes, but funnily, no one noticed this attribute, not even his family, until his recent cancer diagnosis. Whether they had been like that the whole time, or the sickness changed the features of his face to make them more noticeable, is uncertain. Maybe it takes a harsh reminder of the morbidity of life to really see and appreciate the person standing before you.

Suzanne was still trying to get an answer on getting a sample of blood taken from Mario. After nearly losing him, the need to get him tested was even more pressing. Each nurse that Suzanne had spoken to said the same thing: they weren't sure and would ask someone with more authority. Each time, though, the message would get lost and nothing would be done.

When afternoon came and Mario was still stable, Matthew and Suzanne left to go back home to their families in Bunbury. Maria and Stephanie stayed, luckily finding accommodation in the family rooms on the top floor of the hospital. Over the next few days, Mario's seizures stopped and he became less agitated. He was still difficult to understand but if the family and nurses listened carefully they could catch snippets of clear speech, connecting those words together to form a response that hopefully matched what he was trying to say.

Back home, Suzanne received a phone call from Tricia Heaton, a lady from the genetic services. She was returning Suzanne's anxious message left days earlier. Suzanne was able to tell Tricia exactly what was happening and the predicament the family were in, and in turn, Tricia promised to send a fax to the hospital, requesting a sample of blood to be taken from Mario. Suzanne relayed this information back to the family, all relieved that they could finally have Mario tested.

The question now was would Mario improve, or was this how he would be for the remainder of his life? A few more days passed, and as they did, Mario's progress seemed promising, enough so that Stephanie returned home, leaving only Maria to support him. Mario expressed the urge to open his bowels finally; he had spent days without food but now they were feeding him a liquid diet through a feeding tube. The nurse gave him something to help soften his stools and make it easier for him to go but this seemed to work too well, causing him to have uncontrollable diarrhoea. All dignity was lost as he reverted back to the helplessness of a baby, unable to get up and go to the toilet, instead making a mess in his bed.

The nurses couldn't keep up. No sooner had they got him up and changed the bedding and gown, which was a lengthy process, he would do it again. There were times when the nurses were busy and the mess couldn't be cleaned straight away. For a grown man to sit in his own filth, unable to do anything about it, is a crushing and humiliating experience. It was almost a blessing that Mario's brain injury would save him the embarrassment of remembering. Eventually, to solve the problem, a tube was inserted up his rectum, meaning he could go as much as he needed without making a mess.

On the 23rd of February Mario made an impressive leap in his recovery. He was moved out of the High Dependency Unit and into a private room. The physiotherapists had him up on his feet for a short time, he had some feeling return to his left arm, and his speech was getting clearer. This was a big improvement, compared to the condition he was in only a week before. He still had tubes coming out of everywhere and was unable to eat solid foods, but he was still getting a liquid diet through the tube up his nose. Until he could swallow properly the tube would remain. Mario had lost his independence in the blink of an eye, and now the four walls of the hospital room would be his home indefinitely.

The next day was Mario and Maria's wedding anniversary. They never really celebrated anniversaries, simply acknowledging the fact and getting on with their day. The vows that Maria spoke thirty-seven years before, to be there for Mario in sickness and in health, had never rung truer than for the last couple of weeks.

Maria had been staying with Armando and Connie for the last couple of nights but she needed to get back home, now that things had settled down and Mario was out of any immediate danger. The day after their anniversary, Maria went home, and the number of visitors that Mario had slowly dropped, everyone needing to get back to their daily life. That's the thing about life, it doesn't halt and wait for those who have stumbled and fallen. They are left to catch up in their own time, and the hope was that Mario would be able to catch up, that he could come home and slot back into the family life he loved.

Day by day Mario's speech became clearer and his beaming smile returned, even after all he had been through. In the last days of February, when Suzanne and Emmy visited, he took Emmy's hand and said to her, 'You are a beautiful girl. One of the best. I'll fight for you.' He may have lost many things, but what still remained was his love for his family and the will to fight. His body was weak but his soul was strong.

Throughout that week, Suzanne had been communicating back and forth with Tricia, having encountered obstacle after obstacle in getting a blood sample from Mario. First a nurse said that the fax needed to be sent to the head of pathology and that having it sent to Mario's ward wasn't enough. It needed to be done properly and sent through the correct channels. Tricia then rang and spoke to a doctor, who said it didn't need to be sent to pathology and a phlebotomist could take a sample on her rounds of the ward. Then it turned out that they weren't actually allowed to take blood without Mario's consent and as he wasn't in any condition to verbally or physically sign for approving the test, it would mean they couldn't take his blood until he could give permission. No one knew when he would be of sound mind to do this. Frustration grew, especially as the family knew Mario wanted to get tested. Finally, when Tricia realised that getting blood from Mario was not going to happen, she called Suzanne and gave her some good news. They would forget about trying to get Mario's blood, and go straight to testing the willing children. An appointment was organised for Suzanne to get tested, and Tricia explained that if she came back positive, then they would know for certain that Mario was a carrier. If the test came back negative, they would never know if Mario was a carrier, because his children would have a fifty/fifty chance of inheriting the gene. He could still be a carrier, but the children were just lucky enough to not have the gene passed on. Matthew still didn't want to get tested, and Stephanie decided to wait and see what Suzanne's results were. She was still young and had time to decide whether to find out or not. From the age of thirty onwards is when the risk increases dramatically, which is why Suzanne was keen to hurry things along. The family knew that Mario would be pleased if the issue had been taken care of, and all they could hope was that the test would come back negative. They didn't need another reminder of how cruel cancer can be, this disease seemingly infiltrating the Spinelli side, as stealth-like as a vengeful army focused on bringing down as many victims as possible.

After two weeks of being at Sir Charles Gairdner, Mario was transferred to Osborne Park Hospital, where he could begin extensive physiotherapy and occupational therapy. The intention was to transfer him to Fiona Stanley Hospital, but there were no beds available, so Osborne Park was the next choice. At about 1:30pm on the 2nd of March, Mario arrived at his new place of residence and was set up in a shared room. The duration of this stay was still unknown, it all depended on how well Mario continued to progress. All the tubes had been taken out, except for the catheter. His swallowing had improved so he was now able to eat the normal hospital food, but was still at risk of choking so hard foods were not allowed. The physiotherapists came twice a day, getting him to do exercises with his left arm and hand, and helping him walk down the corridors. The occupational therapist put a pen in his hand and asked him to complete a set of activities, like writing his name and address and copying a picture. His right hand was still weak and the effort it took to complete these simple tasks tired him out. The days were long for Mario – family mostly came up on weekends so most of the time was spent on his own. He shared a room with a complete stranger and felt separated from the outside world. He was always tired, whole days spent either in his chair or in his bed. He could remember things, but at the same time was forgetful, memories mixing together in a muddle. His family could see improvements in some areas, like being able to feed himself again, walk short distances, and go to the toilet. But it was still hit and miss, and was evident when the family came to visit and it was clear he had had an accident in bed. A stench lingering in the room, wet clothes in a bag on the floor, Mario wearing a top that clearly didn't belong to him, the buttons straining to stay together, his belly hanging out. The severe trauma to his brain had left its mark, and simple tasks, like going to the toilet, was now an effort in itself. Sadly, pieces of Mario had been lost and it was a very real possibility that they would never be retrieved. He had always loved to talk and could spend hours asking questions, his animated face and kind smile showing just how interested he was. Now, he was quiet, his sentences short, his feelings no longer evident. He sat staring into the distance, and one could only imagine the thoughts going through his head.

On the 11th of March, the doctors took Mario for another CT scan, and Maria rang them the following week to hear what they had found. The specialists had wanted to have another look at the clots on the liver, as they had started him on a lower dose of blood thinners. They didn't say anything new about the cancer, but they were planning to get in touch with his oncologist. There was a possibility of Mario getting discharged on the 23rd March, the doctors saying he may even be able to come straight home, instead of going back to the Bunbury Hospital. But then Maria spoke to Mario's occupational therapist and she said that they had had a meeting about Mario and they thought he needed to spend some time at the Bunbury Hospital. She told Maria that Mario had difficulty comprehending more than one instruction at a time and he still found some words difficult to say. It was clear that there was still a long way to go, that Mario's future had been dramatically altered. There was so much uncertainty and fear of making long-term plans; the only way to get through was to take each day at a time, and hope that Mario could come home to Bunbury soon, so he could spend his days with his family.

He was certainly living on borrowed time now. His body was weakening and wilting from the inside, like a flower, once brilliant and bright, now slowly dying in degrees. The day and date and time that Mario's body would give up the fight was unknown, but at the back of everyone's minds was the knowledge that it could very well be upon them sooner rather than later, and no amount of forethought could prepare them for such a loss.

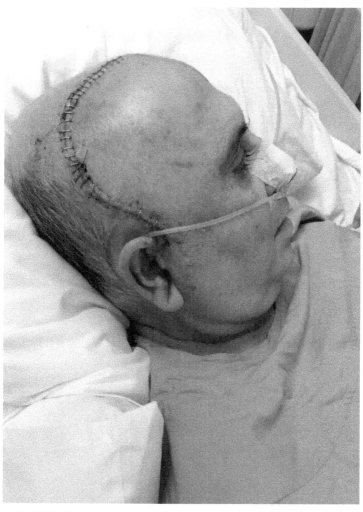

ABOVE: The impressive wound, two days after Mario's lifesaving surgery at Sir Charles Gairdner Hospital, 20th February, 2016.

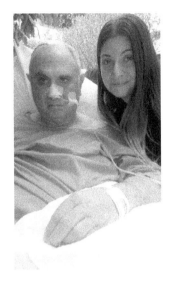
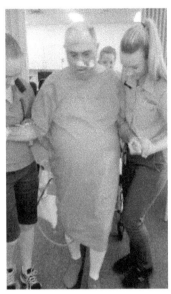

TOP LEFT: *An expressionless Mario, with Stephanie, after his brain surgery, 21ˢᵗ February, 2016.*

TOP RIGHT: *Against all odds, Mario is up on his feet again, 23ʳᵈ February, 2016.*

ABOVE LEFT: *Out of the High Dependency Unit and in his own private room, with Matthew, 27ᵗʰ February, 2016.*

ABOVE RIGHT: *A tired Mario, with Suzanne and Emmy, 28ᵗʰ February, 2016.*

13

Home is Like Heaven

For once, something went to plan, and Mario was transferred from Osborne Park Hospital on the 23rd of March. He was transported in a patient transfer bus to the Restorative Unit at Bunbury Regional Hospital, arriving at about 11:00am. The unit looks after patients who have had serious health issues and require rehabilitation. They work to get the patient to live independently again after episodes that required hospitalisation. The ward and room appeared brighter than the two hospitals Mario had stayed at in Perth, newer and fresher. He was ecstatic to be back in Bunbury, and even though it wasn't quite home, he was one step closer, which was good enough for him. It could have just been that over time Mario was getting stronger and better, but it seemed that his whole demeanour changed when he came back to Bunbury. His smile stretched a little wider, his eyes shone a little brighter, his step got a little quicker.

He still had to have physio and speech therapy; they were working him hard in the hope to get him home as soon as possible. Mario was able to spend a few hours away from the hospital, at first thinking he could go back home for the day. But when the occupational therapists heard that there were some stairs at home, they said it was not a good idea. They hadn't done any work with Mario on stairs, and didn't want to risk an accident. So Maria picked Mario up on Easter Saturday and took him to a café. He was back in the outside world, enjoying a meal that wasn't hospital food, and surrounded by his family. Mario appreciated every moment.

On the 30th March, he had to go back to Sir Charles Gairdner for a haematologist appointment. Maria arrived at the hospital as the new day was dawning and drove him to Perth. The appointment was in relation to the clots in his liver. The doctor explained to them that even though they believed it was the blood thinning drugs that caused the brain bleed, he still needed to be on them to control the clots. In the doctor's words, he was 'stuck between a rock and a hard place'. Without the blood thinners, Mario could develop more life-threatening blood clots. With the blood thinners he had a chance of developing another bleed. All they could do was hope that the latter never happened.

On the 1st of April, the doctor came with some good news. He told Mario that he could be discharged the following Tuesday. From the smile on Mario's face, anyone would think he had just won the lottery.

At least things felt like they were progressing now – that same day, the occupational therapist went to Mario and Maria's house to look at what parts of the house would need railings. She took Mario with her, so she could get him to lie on his bed and chair and toilet, to get an idea of how he would need help using these. After almost seven long weeks of being away from home, Mario finally got to step inside his house, and even though it was only for a short while, it gave him reason to hope, for he could now see the end of living in the hospital, and coming back to the place where he belonged.

That weekend, Mario was let out again for a few hours,

going to Matthew's house on Saturday for morning tea, and Suzanne's house on Sunday for lunch. If they could forget the past couple months and the sadness those thoughts conjured, they could almost pretend that things were normal again.

The day before Mario came home for good, the maintenance man came and installed rails in the bathroom and on the outside step. The house was now set up for Mario's return and he felt such relief, knowing he could finally come home. On the 5th of April, he woke extra happy, for that was the day he could leave the confines of the hospital room and re-join the world, and more importantly, his family. When Maria came to pick him up the nurses went through the discharge process and once the formality of that was over, the staff said goodbye to Mario, telling him they would miss him. Mario and Maria thanked the nurses, hugging them in recognition of the help they had given Mario. Then he walked out of the hospital, not looking back.

At home, Stephanie, Suzanne and Emmy were waiting to greet him. Weeks before, when he'd been at death's door, not looking like he would ever make it back home, this moment seemed unfathomable. Now, here he was, walking independently up the step and through the door into the place he loved most. He smiled widely, and said, 'Home, sweet home.' For Mario, nothing was sweeter than this moment, this opportunity to be back with his family. With his will to live and his fighting spirit, he fought his way back from the brink of death, thankful that he overcame yet another hurdle. To him, being back home was 'like being in Heaven.'

The next step, now that he was back home, was to think about starting treatment again. He saw his oncologist again on the 11th of April, and she said that they would resume treatment the following week, giving him the same drugs but with the amounts adjusted, seeing as he now weighed less than when he was last in. A CAT scan was needed, and she stressed that if the results came back worse, they wouldn't know whether it was because he hadn't responded to treatment or because of the long break from treatment. They would use the latest results as a baseline. She seemed to think Mario would cope with chemotherapy, as he had most of his mobility back, and that the break shouldn't have affected his prognosis too much. The CAT scan results would tell the full story, though, and Mario was able to get the scan that very day. They would find out the results the following week and he would re-start treatment on the 18th. Mario was not keen, but knew if he didn't he 'would really die.'

That was the thing about Mario, he never complained about the situation he was in, never asked 'why me?' He just took what life threw at him and dealt with it. Giving up was not an option and he would do whatever it took to fight. If he had learned anything over the many years he had spent unwell, it was that there was no point in stressing and being negative. He started off like that and soon learnt it just made things worse. So he re-trained his brain, an incredibly difficult thing to do, and determined he would be positive and view the world with an optimistic attitude. This attitude may well have played an important part in him getting through his latest ordeal. When he lay helpless in bed, unable to talk or move, his mind still worked. He could hear himself mumble and moan but all the while he still hoped to overcome this battle. Faith played a part too. When Suzanne was talking to him, saying how lucky he was to have survived this, he simply smiled and said, 'God saved me.' Mario believed he was saved from death that first night of the bleed by a miracle from God that gave him more time on this earth. There had certainly been many times over the years where it could have been it for Mario. He was like a cat with nine lives, and just kept on bouncing back, not quite done with life. But with the cancer, there was going to be a time when he wouldn't bounce back. The day would come when his body, riddled with the insidious disease, would not be able to fight any longer. But for the time being, his fighting spirit and his never-give-up attitude were a source of inspiration and admiration for all his family.

TOP: *Mario has found his smile again, at Osborne Park Hospital, 5th March, 2016.*

ABOVE: *Emmy holds Mario's hand as he slowly walks the hospital corridor, 20th March, 2016.*

LEFT: *One step closer to being home, at the Restorative Unit at Bunbury Regional Hospital, 23rd March, 2016.*

*ABOVE: Happy to finally be home and enjoying Maria's cooking again,
5th April, 2016.*

14

A Second Chance

Two months previously, Mario had lain in a hospital bed, fighting for his life. To see the state he was in, no one would have believed he would survive. Yet here he was, walking unaided into the Bunbury Hospital, ready to re-start his chemotherapy treatment. This moment was lost on the strangers who went about their business, oblivious to the miracle that was in their presence. They would have seen a man walking slowly but surely, his hair clipped a little shorter on one side than the other. They would have seen him smiling, maybe overheard him talking to his wife and daughter, who were walking on either side of him. As with any stranger that we pass in the street, their stories are unknown to us. No one could have known the horror that Mario had recently been through and the improbability of him being alive, let alone being fit enough to undergo chemotherapy treatment.

The moment wasn't lost on Mario, Maria and Suzanne as they sat down in the oncology clinic to wait to see his doctor. But it was also a nervous time, for Mario would be receiving his CAT scan results, and they would finally know whether those months of no treatment had given the cancer a chance to spread further. They didn't have to wait too long, as a door opened and Mario's oncologist ushered them into her room. They all took a seat, and looked expectantly at her, as she looked at Mario's results on the computer.

'Some good news,' she began. 'The cancer has remained stable. Your markers have gone up slightly – they were sixteen before your brain bleed and are now eighteen. Considering your markers were eighty before you started your first treatment, this is good.'

Mario sat up a little straighter and Maria and Suzanne exhaled the air they had been holding inside their chests. One miracle had already befallen Mario. Two seemed even more unlikely, but this news meant Mario would have more time with his family.

The doctor went on to explain that Mario would resume his treatment, with his weekly infusions and three-weekly chemotherapy treatments, starting that day. While waiting for the nurses to call him in for treatment, he turned to Suzanne and said, 'I have a feeling I'll get through this.' Optimistic, as always.

The nurses were happy to see Mario's smiling face back on the ward, and asked him where he had been over the last few months.

'Did you get sick of us already?' one nurse joked.

Mario laughed heartily, and then told her the full story.

Shaking her head, she said, 'Sounds like you have had a rough time lately.'

That was an understatement. 'It's lucky you are still here with us,' she finished.

It was more than luck, it was a miracle.

Not long after Mario had been hooked up to his chemotherapy, a lady from Pastoral Care came by to say hello. She had visited Mario when he first started having treatment, but it took him a little while to remember her. She asked him how he had been, and he told her briefly about what had happened. She also shook her head, then looking up, she said, 'Someone was looking out for you, Mario.' People often say that as a passing comment, one that isn't really believed by the person making the statement, but rather to show how lucky they were in avoiding disaster. But Mario nodded and smiled genuinely, firmly believing that he had truly been looked after, his faith even more solid than before.

The session was long, and while Maria and Suzanne chatted together and waited, Mario hung his head and slept. He still tired easily, his body working to re-gain the strength he had lost. When he woke, the treatment was almost over.

The next day, a nurse from the community Palliative Care team came to visit Mario. The service was arranged by the hospital and was designed for cancer patients and their carers who might need support from home. Mario wasn't keen on the idea at first, saying to Maria, 'Darling, I feel fine now. I don't need them coming here to remind me I'm sick.' It made the family uneasy too, the word 'palliative' reminding them that there was only one outcome to Mario's situation. But the nurse eased their minds somewhat, saying that they started the visits now to get to know Mario's situation and to provide them with information about what they can offer to him and his family, especially as the disease starts progressing further. She also provided some hope, explaining that she too was a cancer survivor, even though she had been given a timeframe of only a few years to live. Yet here she was, many years later, and cancer-free. Life is a guessing game, a wait-and-see, a gamble. But the odds weren't in Mario's favour. He told the nurse his wishes so the Community Palliative team knew what they needed to do when the time came. Mario's main wish was to die at home. The nurse assured him that they would do all they could to obey his wishes. She explained that, from now on, she or other palliative care nurses would visit periodically, touching base and seeing how he and the family were coping.

The following week, Maria drove Mario to the Australind Jetty. Suzanne had organised for her photographer friend to come down and take some family photos. A chance to capture Mario with his family, together in that moment, happy and whole, before anything more could happen.

Mario looked smart, wearing a blue button-down collared shirt, with black dress pants and shoes. He was cleanly shaven, his crucifix necklace visible over his shirt. Even with his belt on, his pants were still loose, threatening to fall down if he wasn't careful.

It was a sunny day in April, the backdrop peaceful; a few wispy clouds painted across a clear blue sky, ripples on the water, over-hanging trees casting lazy shadows on the crisp grass. There was laughter and snippets of conversation in between the clicks of the camera, Mario enjoying his time in front of the camera and amongst his family. The camera captured Mario's pale, smiling face, his dark eyes and the loose flesh on his arms. But most of all, it captured him, evidence that he was alive and present, and still fighting.

After the photo shoot, Mario and Maria went back home, followed by Matthew, Suzanne and Stephanie. The fun was over; now it was time for more serious matters. The family had organised with Mario to sit down and have a conversation with him, to discuss the finer details of his last wishes. A morbid conversation, but a necessary one, as the family didn't want to get caught out again.

Suzanne was the scribe, pen and paper at the ready to document Mario's thoughts. Over cups of steaming tea, his family listened as he spoke. He talked calmly, as if the topic was an ordinary one. He appeared to have no trouble talking about the details of his funeral, and about who would have his beloved tools once he was no longer there to use them. When he was done, he smiled, relieved that this time, he had the chance to express what he wanted, to have taken back some control over his situation.

Another situation that they all had no control over was the BRCA1 gene that resided in some members of the Spinelli family. But in the last week of April, Suzanne's appointment to have her blood test finally came. It was going to be a long wait for results, usually taking two months to find the outcome. Once those results came in, though, they would finally have a little control over something. If positive, they would have that knowledge to help Suzanne take steps to prevent probable cancer. If positive, they would know that Mario was a carrier, making it even more important for Stephanie to be tested. Mario had decided there was no point in getting himself tested, as it was too late for him and there would be no benefit to knowing. His daughters were able to get tested themselves, so he was just happy to leave it at that. He hoped with all his heart that Suzanne's results would come back negative.

As with everything else, they just had to wait and see.

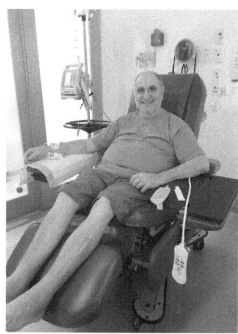

LEFT: *Mario resumes his treatment, 18th April, 2016.*

ABOVE: *Blessed to have more time with his beloved family, from left to right – Abbey, Matthew, Mario, Maria, Stephanie, Suzanne, Jordan, Emmy, and at front, Jesaia and Coby, 23rd April, 2016. (Photograph by Jessica Mill Photography)*

15

A Time for Celebration

The next couple of months were worthy of celebration, as there were many things for Mario to smile about. For one, Mario's sixty-fifth birthday was approaching. For him to be celebrating another birthday was surreal, considering only months before, he had been close to death. Unbeknown to him, Maria had planned a surprise party. The event was low-key, taking place on the 1st of May, at a local restaurant with only his closest family and friends attending. Mario thought he was going out to lunch with only his immediate family, as that is what Maria had told him. So when he walked through the door and saw the room full of his extended family, his heart swelled as he realised they were all there for him. The look on his face was priceless – eyes wide and mouth open, his surprise and elation evident. He turned to Maria and embraced her, then faced his audience, scanning the room with a broad smile lighting up his face. Family members clapped and cheered, and then, one by one, they went to Mario to say hello and gave him hugs, gifts and birthday wishes. Mario enjoyed the afternoon, eating a nice meal and talking to his family. It was days like these that made him even more thankful that he was alive.

On Mario's actual birthday, the 3rd of May, Maria cooked a hearty dinner, this time only inviting their immediate family, plus Gina and Catena. They shared cake leftover from the party, and watched eagerly as Mario opened his present. It was a framed family portrait, from when they had their photos taken at the Australind Jetty.

Mario looked at it for a few moments, then said, 'Ah, thank you. I love it. I'll treasure this one.'

The photo, now framed and on display, signified so much more; it was family, standing together, after everything they had been through, with Mario still the proud patriarch.

Since returning home from hospital, he had been attending both physio and speech therapy sessions and showing considerable improvement. In fact, Mario was mostly back to the way he was before the brain bleed. So, much to his relief, he attended his last session on the 5th of May. Thankfully, he didn't need therapy for the rest of his life, which had been a real possibility when the trauma to his brain first occurred. He was back to his old self, as talkative as ever. He had certainly made up for those few weeks when he couldn't speak properly, and now he wasn't wasting his ability to talk freely. This was the Mario that everyone knew and loved.

It had been almost three weeks since Mario's last chemotherapy and he was due for another round. The routine blood test that he had before each treatment showed his white cell count was low, so chemotherapy was postponed. He was still able to have his infusion, but his white cell count would need to be higher before chemotherapy was given.

On the 7th June, Maria and Matthew took Mario to visit his sister, Josephine. The drive took a few hours, but Mario felt well enough to travel there for the day. Josephine also suffers from a number of health issues and had been unable to visit

Mario in hospital. She had remained very anxious about her brother, and was now eager to find out how he was going. Because of both Mario and Josephine's health problems, they hadn't seen each other in a very long time. It was a happy reunion; the two siblings who had shared a close bond in childhood were now together again, if only for a few hours.

The rest of June passed uneventfully, but there were two more reasons to celebrate. The first was that Suzanne received her BRCA1 result. The family was elated to learn that it was negative. It still didn't answer the question about Mario being a carrier, but for Mario to hear that his eldest daughter didn't have the cancer gene was a welcome relief. One less thing to worry about was always a good thing.

The second reason for celebration was that Mario had another CAT scan, and it showed that his cancer hadn't progressed much further and was still stable. It is funny how crazy things can get, how hopeless things can seem, but once the storm has passed, life has a way of returning to the everyday normalcy that came before. This was how it was for Mario, who had slipped back into life as if nothing terrible had happened previously. Even though the cancer still resided in his body, it was quiet for now, letting him enjoy the life he loved living.

Scan this QR code to watch a video of Mario's 65th Birthday Surprise.
Or visit:
www.suzifaed.com/surprise-birthday/

TOP: Mario's surprise 65th birthday celebrations, from left to right –
Abbey, Matthew, Suzanne, Mario, Stephanie, Jordan and Maria,
2nd May, 2016.

ABOVE: A long-awaited reunion, Mario and his sister, Josephine,
7th June, 2016.

16

The Calm Before the Storm

Life was well and truly back to normal, and days went by uneventfully. On the 2nd of July, Mario went to Mandurah for two nights with Maria, Stephanie, Jordan, Suzanne, Emmy, Gina and Catena. They had rented a classy, modern home on the canals, and were looking forward to a weekend of relaxation.

'Ah,' Mario breathed as he stepped into the house for the first time. 'This is beautiful. Beats staying at home all the time!' Mario enjoyed every moment of being together with his family, and was glad he felt well enough to accompany them on a walk along the Mandurah foreshore, the beach and also a visit to the Zoo. A long time ago, when Mario was trapped in his darkest days, he would never have joined them on family outings, instead opting to stay home and sleep. He would have given up before he started, saying he was too tired and weak to walk around. But the new Mario, the one who chose to fight, was now walking alongside his family, making memories that they would be happy to look back on in years to come. Not once did he complain that he was tired. He had been reminded first-hand about the fragility of life;

now he wasn't going to waste the rest of his days sitting around doing nothing.

Mario's weekly infusions were going well. It was fortunate they were working, as he had missed out on chemotherapy for a while. A common side effect from the infusion, though, was that skin can become sensitive and Mario developed an angry, spotty rash on his face and arms. His hands were chaffed and sore, splits forming in the folds of his fingers, making it hard to use his hands. When the rash wouldn't go away, Mario's oncologist put him on antibiotics and gave him a week off from his treatment. Slowly, the rash faded and his hands improved, to Mario's relief.

On the 1st of August, Mario received another visit from the community Palliative nurse. She was a different nurse to the one who had visited previously, so in getting to know Mario's situation, she asked what the outlook was for him. Maria reiterated what Mario's oncologist had told them about his prognosis, being one year without treatment, and two years with.

Later, when the nurse had left, Mario went to Maria and asked, 'About my prognosis, who told you that?'

Maria answered, 'The doctor told us, on your first visit.'

Seemingly unaffected, Mario simply responded with, 'Well, I'd better get all my jobs done then. But I'll still be positive.'

The family had suspected that Mario hadn't fully grasped the outlook for his situation, based on a number of comments he had made along the way. They'd thought that surely he had some idea; either that or he truly hadn't understood, or was in denial. That his positivity was due to the fact that he still believed he had a chance of beating the cancer. But after Mario heard his prognosis, that he may possibly only have another two years to live, he still chose to remain positive. His acceptance of what life threw at him, his knowledge that it was out of his control, helped him accept and process the news. 'This is life,' he told Suzanne one day. 'What can we do?'

As the weeks progressed, he still hadn't been able to have chemotherapy, as each blood test showed that his white cell count remained low. It was normal for the white cell count to be low after a chemotherapy session, but not normal for it to continuously stay low, especially since Mario's last chemotherapy session was four months before. Whenever he would visit his oncologist, she would mention his result and say they would try again next week. But when it was clear that the white cells weren't improving, the oncologist referred him to a haematologist.

When Maria asked the doctor why she thought Mario's white cells were not increasing, she responded with, 'I have an inkling of why they're low, but I can't say. The haematologist will be able to confirm why.'

The appointment was booked for the 24th of October, so until then, it would remain a mystery to Mario and Maria.

On the 4th of September, the nation celebrated Father's Day. Mario felt blessed in both being a father and in still being alive to celebrate the day. His beloved children could easily have been visiting his grave if things had turned out differently, but as it was, they got to visit him in the flesh, and took the opportunity to tell him how proud they were of him and how he had handled everything he had been through. Growing up, they hadn't seen the man he was, but over the past few years especially, he had shown them what it took to truly be brave and strong in hardship. This day had much more meaning than any other Father's Day gone by, and they all tried to ignore the thought that this could be his last, instead focusing on the fact that he was here for this one.

The next day, Mario had another CAT scan. It was important that they were done regularly to keep track of what the cancer was doing. Thankfully, when the results came back, it showed the cancer was still stable, much the same as the last scan. Mario was still winning this fight, his stubborn nature having its benefits. There would be a time when the scan would show different results, when the sighs of relief would turn to sighs of resignation, when the scans would set in motion the beginning of a harsh, new reality. But that was for the future. Until then, Mario and his family would enjoy the calm before the storm.

Meanwhile, Mario kept busy by working in his sheds. A man's dream, he had two sheds – the main, large one, and a smaller garden shed adjacent to it. He also had a small storage room downstairs, in the garage. For many years they had all been neglected, allowing spiders to build their cobwebs, for tools to lay unused, layers of dust forming on every surface. The sheds had acted as storage space, Mario collecting and hoarding tools he said he 'needed and would use one day.' That day seemed to never come, and as a result, his sheds were cluttered and unworkable.

But Mario was feeling good, and while he was motivated and able to work, he did. He started on his garden shed, first getting Matthew and Jordan to help pull everything out and discard anything that would be of no use, which was most of it. His hoarding came in handy, though, as he had a number of long pieces of wood that had been taking up space in his big shed for years. He decided he would use them to make shelves for the garden shed. This kept him busy for a number of hours each day, and sometimes he would spend the whole day out there, only coming in for lunch. He was very satisfied when that job was complete, having now turned the garden shed into practical storage space. His hands hadn't lost the ability to create, and his mind still held the knowledge that he had learned as a young man. His left arm and hand, not long ago paralysed, were now able to hold his tools and do what he was good at. His mental illness, his cancer, and his brain bleed couldn't take that away from him.

Next he started on the big shed, also tidying and discarding. And finally the little storage room in the downstairs garage, doing the same. Mario hadn't worked this much in years, and it pleased him that he was feeling well enough to do so. There is nothing like a near-death experience to make you get your affairs in order, and to Mario, cleaning out his sheds made him feel organised and back in control. For years, he would say he would get to the jobs. There was always tomorrow. He would do it later. When he felt better. But now he knew that his tomorrows were running out. Rather than allowing it to depress him, he used it to spur him on and to ensure that he didn't waste any of his todays.

TOP LEFT: *Enjoying a little getaway in Mandurah,*
from front – Jordan, Suzanne, Catena,
back – Stephanie, Gina, Maria, Emmy and Mario, 3rd July, 2016.

TOP RIGHT *&* ABOVE RIGHT: *Mario feeling well and working in*
his shed, 13th July, 2016.

ABOVE LEFT: *Mario preparing a shelf for his shed, 17th July, 2016.*

17

Waiting and Worrying

In late September, Mario's routine blood tests showed that his cancer markers had begun to increase. These markers were used as a guide to get an idea of what the disease was doing. Previously, Mario's markers remained stable, after having decreased as a result of his Cetuximab infusions. The markers had hovered around four for quite a while, but were now seven. Only an increase of three, but an indication that the cancer had possibly become active again.

Things seemed to go from bad to worse, when Mario attended the haematologist appointment on the 24th October. The doctor was from Perth, but had an office in Bunbury from which she practiced every couple of months. She had a kind, warm manner and welcomed Mario and Maria into her office with a genuine smile. But what she had to say soon changed the atmosphere of the room; her thoughts of what was wrong with Mario were not positive at all. Based on the information she had received from Mario's oncologist, she had deduced that there could be a number of possible reasons for Mario's low white cell count. The first was cancer infiltration – that the cancer in the liver had spread to the bone marrow, therefore making it unable to produce more white cells. The second was a condition called Myelodysplasia, a disease most commonly found in older people, which affect the normal blood cell production in the bone marrow. She also mentioned the possibility of fibrosis, a condition that caused scarring of the liver, but said that that was unlikely. Of course, the reason could also be one she had not yet thought of. Her reasons were only educated guesses and the only way to find out for sure was to have a bone marrow test. This would indicate whether the bone marrow contained cancer cells. If not, then at least it would rule out the possibility.

Unfortunately the doctor was fully booked that day, otherwise Mario could have had the test there and then. The next time the doctor would be in Bunbury was the 5th of December – a six-week wait. Mario could get an earlier appointment if they went to Perth, but he didn't want to have to travel up there. So the appointment was booked for December and yet again, Mario prepared to wait for answers regarding his health. When they relayed the information back to his family, all agreed that it would be better to just drive to Perth if it meant getting an answer sooner.

'But Darling,' Mario said to Maria, 'I can't hack the trip up. Being in the car makes me feel funny.'

Suzanne stepped in. 'If it means getting an answer sooner, and being able to figure out where to go with your treatment sooner, don't you think it will be worth it? I'll come with you guys if it makes you feel better.'

Mario looked at Maria for a second, then back to Suzanne. 'All right, you've convinced me. I would love it if you came with us.'

And just like that, Mario's mind was changed, easily swayed by his family's concern.

Maria called to change the appointment and was able to get one for the 9th of November. It was only a two-week wait, and less time for everyone to mull over the depressing diagnoses the doctor had come up with.

The day before the Perth appointment, Mario had another visit with his oncologist. When he last saw her his markers had been seven. They had increased again, and were now ten, slowly creeping up. Rising gradually, like a sleeping snake coming out of hibernation, sluggish after lying dormant for so long but preparing to strike again and with enough powerful venom to kill at any time.

This information didn't seem promising, along with the fact that Mario's white cells had remained low for months now. But when the doctor told Mario and Maria of the increase, Mario misinterpreted the news and thought the rise was positive.

'That's good, Doctor,' Mario said enthusiastically, to which the doctor looked at him and replied with, 'No, it's not good.'

It was time for a PET scan and a CAT scan, so the doctor wrote a request form for the two, and also mentioned that Mario's magnesium levels were down, so he would be receiving magnesium intravenously, along with his normal infusion. It was unusual that these were low, as he was already on two tablets twice a day.

After Mario had his Cetuximab and magnesium infusion, he and Maria left to book his scans. They weren't able to get an appointment until the 28th November, so as always, it would be a matter of waiting and worrying.

18

The Bone Marrow Test

It was time for Mario's bone marrow test. He woke on the morning of the 9th of November, ready and eager to have the procedure. Maria drove to Perth, with Mario humming happily in the passenger seat and Suzanne nervously sitting in the back. Both Maria and Suzanne had heard that a bone marrow test could be extremely uncomfortable – a needle going all the way through to the hipbone would surely be painful.

They had time to spare before the appointment so they enjoyed a coffee in the hospital café. Mario wasn't nervous at all and when the doctor opened her door and called his name, Maria and Suzanne's stomachs flipped, but Mario strode into the room, beaming a bright smile at the doctor. She greeted the trio; they sat down, and listened as the doctor briefly reiterated the reason for testing Mario's bone marrow. She mentioned another reason, stating that his white cells could have been affected by the chemotherapy he had. The powerful drugs could have destroyed the marrow, meaning it couldn't recover. Mario hadn't had too many chemotherapy sessions, so it was hard to imagine that this could be the cause. Nonetheless, it was worrying because if that was found to be the reason, then Mario would have no hope of ever re-starting chemotherapy again. As if this wasn't enough, the doctor raised another possibility – leukaemia. She was doubtful, but she felt she needed to be clear with the family. The message was certainly received loud and clear by Maria and Suzanne.

Taking a deep breath, Suzanne asked, 'So, if the cancer is in the marrow, will that affect Dad's prognosis?'

The doctor nodded, and with sympathy in her voice, said, 'Yes, it will shorten his prognosis.'

With that said, Mario sliced through the heaviness in the room, and bravely hopped onto the bed. 'I'm ready, Doctor.'

As the doctor prepared her instruments, she ran through the information about the procedure and what to expect. Then she instructed Mario to lie on his side, with his knees bent. She cleaned the area and injected some local anaesthetic where the needle would pierce his skin.

Waiting a couple of minutes for the anaesthetic to work, the doctor then said, 'Okay, Mario, are you ready?'

'Yes,' he replied confidently. 'I'm ready, Doctor.'

She went carefully, slowly inserting the needle through Mario's skin. Through flesh, tissue, then muscle – the sharp needle found its mark in Mario's bone.

From the centre of the bone, the doctor sucked the bone marrow back into the needle. This was where the procedure was supposed to be painful. This was where patients normally felt a sharp, sudden, pulling sensation. But Mario lay completely still, at ease and comfortable.

'Can you feel this at all, Mario?'

'I can feel it but I can bear it, Doctor.'

Mario was always full of surprises, never doing anything by the book, but it was a relief that the procedure went well and didn't cause Mario too much discomfort.

Now, with Mario's marrow sitting inside a testing tube,

awaiting the microscope, an appointment was booked for the 5th of December to find out exactly what was going on.

As Mario, Maria and Suzanne walked out of the doctor's office, Suzanne congratulated Mario on how brave he was, and for getting through another procedure. As always, Mario smiled and had something positive to say. Even with none of the options the doctor mentioned being positive, Mario still talked of beating his disease.

'I hope it goes into remission and I can live with it!'

As much as the family loved his bright outlook, it saddened them to know that there was only one absolute with terminal cancer. So this statement sat heavy on Maria and Suzanne's heart, but then Mario said, 'We'll stop and have something to eat and talk about how courageous I was.'

They laughed, the mood lightened for a moment. Tension eased, as bone marrow tests and results were forgotten and they became just another family looking to share lunch together.

*

The next day, as Mario pottered around the house, his mind was obviously thinking back to his visit to the doctor the day before. Sometimes Mario missed things, or misinterpreted them, because he was hard of hearing.

He went and found Maria and asked, 'Darling, what did the doctor say?'

Maria didn't have the heart to go through all the depressing options with him again, so she responded with, 'She's not one hundred-percent sure what is going on so it's best to wait until we get the results. Don't stress about it, we'll see what the doctor has planned when she knows more.'

A part of Mario knew the answer anyway. 'I don't want to

die. I'm too young and I hope God can save me again because I want to see my family grow up.'

'Keep on doing what you're doing and stay positive,' Maria encouraged.

'I will, Darling. I'm always positive.'

ABOVE: Before the bone marrow test, Mario, Suzanne and Maria, 9th November, 2016.

19

Renewed Hope

After a few weeks of waiting for results, the time had come for Mario and his family to receive more answers. Within that time frame, Mario had still been having his Cetuximab and magnesium infusions. He had also seen his oncologist, who had again informed them that Mario's markers were still creeping up. She had the preliminary results from the bone marrow test but said it was best to wait until they saw Mario's haematologist.

Mario, Maria and Suzanne sat in the waiting room, anticipating the doctor's door opening so she could usher them inside and put an end to their wondering. It was mid-morning, on the 5th of December – an otherwise special day as it was Emmy's second birthday. A day when Mario and Maria should have been celebrating with their granddaughter, watching her open presents instead of waiting for more potential heartache.

After a short time, the door opened and the doctor called them in. They each took a seat, greeted the doctor then waited for her to sit at her desk and organise herself.

'Mario, how did you feel after you had the procedure? I don't think you even noticed me do the biopsy, did you?'

'No, everyone was telling me it was going to be very painful. Two days later I still didn't feel any pain at all.'

Maria said, 'He must have a high pain threshold.'

'Yes, I think he does. Now I was expecting to find something not very nice in there but I found the best possible thing that we could find. Your bone marrow is hyperactive and making lots and lots of cells.'

'Oh, that's good news,' Mario said, with relief in his voice.

The doctor continued. 'What is happening is the spleen is enlarged. Because the liver has some disease in it, there is a problem with the blood flow to the liver, and because it's a plumbing system, it's causing pressure in the spleen and the spleen is enlarging. The spleen is just a filter, essentially, and it seems to be holding onto your blood cells and breaking them down.'

Mario was leaning forward, listening intently. 'I see. So that's good news then?'

'Yes, that's actually very good news.'

Maria and Suzanne exhaled. 'Wow,' Maria managed, while Suzanne let out a relieved laugh.

'I was not expecting that. I don't even tell people that's an option because it gets their hopes up and most of the time it's something else, something not very nice. So out of all the possibilities, that's actually the best one because that might be treatable by taking the spleen out.'

'Oh, so does that mean Dad would need to have surgery?' Suzanne asked.

'Yes, we need to eradicate the spleen or somehow reduce the effectiveness of it. So it's not simple to deal with, but it's not a cancerous reason.'

'Yeah, 'cause all the options you gave were not good,' Suzanne added.

'No. And it should mean that chemotherapy shouldn't be so much of an issue as it might have been if the bone marrow wasn't making enough cells properly. Essentially what's happened is that your body's got lots of those cells but they are not in your blood stream. They're effectively being filtered out. When the spleen is enlarged it sort of does its job too well.'

The relief in the room was palpable. After being given reason to think the results would have been bad no matter what, but then getting the opposite, it allowed that seed of hope to grow again. Now they knew what they were dealing with, the next thing was to find out how they could solve the problem and get Mario back on his chemotherapy regime.

The doctor started to explain what options Mario had. 'There are various ways of dealing with it. One would be surgery; one would be radiation. Sometimes there's – I don't think they can do it anymore – they used to try and block off the blood supply and that tends to hurt a lot.'

Suzanne had a question. 'Can he handle surgery, though, with everything going on with him?'

'That would be the surgeon's call.'

'Hmm. That's a worry, too, how he would cope with that.'

'Yes. Essentially, it's up to the oncologist. What she wanted from me was to know if she could give this man chemotherapy. And I think the answer would be yes. But there are a lot of whys and ifs and buts, so of all the possibilities, this is the best one, but it doesn't mean the road from here is simple.'

*

The next day, Mario had an appointment with his oncologist to receive his PET/CAT scan results, and to discuss the issue of his bone marrow. Again, Maria and Suzanne were by his side.

'Hello, Doctor,' Mario said, and proceeded to tell her

what the haematologist had told him, even though she had already seen a report.

She listened, nodding her head, as Mario gave a good summary of the problem.

'When I saw the results I suspected that was what was probably going on. It's something that…let me just go through your results and we'll come back to that. So you had the PET and CAT scan and that shows that things are pretty stable in size. The spleen is big but there's nothing new on the scans, which is good. Compared to the PET scan that you had previously, it shows that the activity in the liver lesion is less, nothing really new, which is good. And those lymph nodes that were there aren't active anymore so that's all good. It doesn't explain why the markers have been trending up but I prefer the results of the scan rather than following the bloods.'

While the doctor spoke, the trio nodded in relief. From the two appointments, things seemed positive. The bone marrow wasn't damaged and the cancer hadn't spread. There was hope – it was just a matter of seeing if removing the spleen would be something that Mario's oncologist would approve.

Now that Mario had received his scan results, he wanted to get back to discussing the possibility of surgery. 'She said it was up to you whether you decide for me to have an operation or not.'

'Look, I think it might be something that is, in the long run, worthwhile. Only because, at the moment, I'm happy to keep going with this medication, but at some point, when it does stop working and things start growing again, we're going to need to use chemotherapy. At the moment we couldn't do that because the counts aren't right. So I think it's something to think about, and start the planning for if you're okay with going for that, and then getting the surgeon to have a look and see what we can do.'

The doctor paused for a moment, then asked, 'Would you be happy if we start that pathway?'

Mario started to nod his head, when Maria asked, 'Would that be too late, if we leave it and not do it straight away?'

The doctor thought about the question for a bit, seemingly trying to find a satisfactory response. 'Well…like I…I don't think…I think we need to plan it. I don't think it needs to be done, like, yesterday. It's not causing you any side effects except for the low count, which haven't caused you any problems so far. But if you do want chemotherapy, then that's the only thing that will help.'

Mario asked, 'So you would like to keep going with the infusion at the moment?'

'Yes, at the moment I think we can continue what we are doing and start the planning.'

'Well, I'm thinking after Christmas, maybe in January.'

'Yes, certainly it's Christmas in a few weeks. We can plan for it and then, when we need to get you back on chemotherapy, we can do it straight away.'

Suzanne had been sitting quietly, listening to the conversation that was taking place. She asked the same question she had asked the day before. 'Is it a big operation? Will he be able to cope with it, do you think?'

'Yes, look, he has coped quite well with everything so far. It's a decent sized operation but these days they make the incision as small as possible.'

'Okay. What do you think the explanation is for Dad's markers going up? Could it be possible that there is cancer growing but the scan didn't pick it up?'

Even though the results had shown things were stable, and Mario was satisfied with what was happening, Suzanne still felt uneasy about the markers that were increasing steadily.

'Not sure. Other things can put the markers up; it's not just the cancer. I mean, it's possible there are things we're not seeing because they are too small but at the moment, we can't see them so we can't say that.'

The family was relieved that the outcome of those two appointments were positive, especially considering the doctors had thought it was likely that Mario's bone marrow had become diseased. The fact that it hadn't, and the scan showed nothing new, felt like a wonderful Christmas present. Mario had renewed hope and believed he had control of his cancer. In late December, along with his normal Cetuximab infusion, he had another magnesium infusion, and an iron infusion – the haematologist had found his iron levels were considerably low and so had instructed his oncologist to give him this as well.

He felt good that last month of 2016. He celebrated Christmas with his family; he enjoyed good food and time spent with his loved ones. It had been a year since his diagnosis, a year since the doctor told him he had between a year and two years to live. For someone who was supposed to be dying, he felt very much alive. He was looking forward to the New Year ahead, not allowing himself to be anything but positive about what was going on. He didn't give a thought to the markers that were increasing inside his body. He felt good, and that, during a festive period spent in the bosom of his family, was all that mattered.

THIS PAGE:
Christmas celebrations with Mario's family, 25th December, 2016.

20

Running Out of Options

For Christmas, Mario had received a colourful garden gnome from Jordan and Suzanne. At first glance, it would have been considered an odd present, for the fact that Mario was not much of a gardener and didn't really have a fine appreciation of the likes of a gnome in his garden. But it wasn't meant for Mario's garden and the gesture was more of a symbolic one. On the back of the gnome, Suzanne had written his name and the year, along with the words *Fighting Spirit*. Those two words held so much meaning – they summarised Mario's journey, the trials he had faced and the brave and courageous way he had fought them. They symbolised his positive and happy nature, the essence of his soul. Those two words captured the example he set for those who knew him and had been inspired by his never-give-up attitude.

Suzanne explained to Mario that together, they would take this gnome to a place called Gnomesville, in Ferguson Valley – a thirty-minute drive from Bunbury. On the 8th of January, 2017, that is what they did. They left mid-morning, the summer sun already giving the air some warmth. Mario dressed in shorts, a shirt and a black, straw hat. He looked healthy and wore a bright smile, as always, having been looking forward to a day out with his family.

They walked along the sandy path that wound its way through Gnomesville, on the lookout for the perfect spot to house Mario's gnome. After about ten minutes, they found an empty spot next to a tall, thin tree. As the cicadas sang their rhythmic song, their beat of soft-clicks providing a steady tune, Mario bent over to place the gnome at the base of the tree. The ground was uneven and the gnome almost toppled over, so he dug into the dry sand, to make a little hole for it to sit in. Mario didn't say a word, and after a few moments he turned the gnome upside down and looked at it, as if it was the gnome's fault it couldn't penetrate the soil.

Gina joked, 'Did anyone bring a spade?'

The others laughed, but Mario was serious about getting his gnome to stay. After a few more attempts, his gnome stood upright.

Mario straightened up too and said, 'There!' with a hint of relief in his voice.

That gnome now resides in that place, nestled under a tree. It is just one gnome out of thousands. Many people have no doubt passed by since that day, some may even have read the message written on the small statue. The words would mean little if anything, their significance washing over the casual tourist who, moving on would forget within seconds. But to Mario and his family, that little gnome was another memory made. It was a reminder that Mario had fought and was continuing to fight. That he had walked that path and left a piece of his existence, proof that he was able to still leave his mark.

*

The following month, on the 8th of February, Mario had an

appointment with the surgeon to discuss the possible removal of his spleen. The surgeon had already met Mario; he was the one who had operated on him to remove his bowel cancer years ago. After the surgeon looked through the notes and externally examined Mario's spleen – which he found to be very enlarged – he asked, 'How are you feeling?'

Mario replied, 'Good!'

The surgeon's eyes widened slightly, just enough to show that he was expecting a different answer, based on what he knew about Mario's case. The surgeon then went on to explain the details of the surgery and Mario expressed that he wanted to have the surgery in Bunbury, and have a keyhole procedure. He didn't want to have to be cut open, knowing that recovery was harder. The surgeon told him that unfortunately, if Mario wanted keyhole surgery, he would have to go to Perth, as they did not do that type of surgery in Bunbury. This disappointed Mario, as he wanted to be close to home, but he felt it was more important to have a less invasive procedure. The surgeon explained that he would need to refer him to another surgeon in Perth, and he would need to attend an appointment up in the city to discuss the surgery with this other doctor. Mario and Maria had been hoping the current appointment would be the one to organise a date for the surgery, so they felt a little frustrated that things were being delayed again. They were told that they would receive a letter with an appointment date, so the best they could do was hope they would hear back from the doctor soon.

Two days later Mario had another PET scan. His routine blood tests showed that his markers were still increasing, and were now forty-one. Normally he wouldn't have needed another scan so soon after the previous one, but his oncologist thought it was required due to the markers rising quite quickly. This time, he didn't have to wait too long for the results. Three days later, on the 13th of February, Mario sat with his oncologist and received news he was not expecting, nor wanting to hear. She explained that his PET scan showed the cancer in his liver was worse, and they also found he had a lymph node near his liver.

'Unfortunately,' she explained, 'this means that the Cetuximab infusion is no longer working. I'm afraid I'll have to stop it as there is no point in continuing if it has lost its effect.'

Mario sat, calm and collected, choosing not to consider what this meant for his prognosis. Maria and Suzanne sat beside him, stunned that this moment was now upon them. They were very aware of the repercussions of ceasing the one drug that had been successfully slowing down the spread of his cancer.

'Where to now?' Maria asked quietly.

'When you have the appointment with the surgeon, we'll know more. If he can have his spleen removed and his white cells go up afterwards, Mario can hopefully resume chemotherapy. If they don't go up, he won't be able to have it. Aside from chemotherapy, there aren't really any more options.'

'That's a lot of *ifs*,' Suzanne said despondently.

The oncologist stood, walking them to the door. 'Make an appointment with me after you have seen the surgeon. We'll go from there. Good luck, Mario.'

They had barely stepped out of the office when Mario was already making it clear he wasn't disheartened by the bad news.

'I'm staying positive, Darling. Once I have my spleen removed, I'll be able to start chemotherapy again.'

Mario chose to pin his hopes on this surgery. He spoke definitively, choosing to leave *ifs* out of his vocabulary. But on that hot day in February, in those minutes spent in the oncologist's office – that was the start of Mario's gradual decline. Mario's disease was no longer stable and treatment was no longer working. He was approaching the last part of his journey, whether he believed it or not.

LEFT: *Mario holding his gnome proudly at Gnomesville, Ferguson Valley, 8th January, 2017.*

RIGHT: *Mario 'planting' his gnome at Gnomesville, Ferguson Valley.*

21

Between a Rock and a Hard Place

Not long after this bad news, Mario started to show physical signs that all was not well within him. Only a week had passed and already he was becoming increasingly tired. He began sleeping for hours during the day and would still have no problem sleeping all night. Apart from feeling tired and lethargic, he otherwise felt well. He would still wake from a deep slumber with a big smile on his face. He would still talk enthusiastically and ask lots of questions and share cups of tea with anyone who would join him. Being around his family seemed to pep him up as well as it ever did. One afternoon, when Suzanne came back from work, she asked him how he was. He told her he had been sleeping all day.

Concerned, Suzanne asked, 'Do you still feel tired?'

'Not anymore. Seeing you has rejuvenated me.'

Yet it wasn't long before some new symptoms began to surface. In the space of another week, Mario had begun to feel itchy all over. His skin and eyes had turned a shade of yellow, he felt weak, his voice was softer and he walked slower. He had some episodes of diarrhoea. He was wilting before his family's eyes but his mind was strong. He was still so hopeful about the spleen surgery and thought this episode of sickness was just another hurdle he would have to overcome.

'I feel sick but I won't give up. There are people worse off than me.'

It was lucky that Mario had such a positive attitude and didn't stress about the unknown or having to wait for answers. He wasn't able to get an appointment with the surgeon until the 14th of March. The wait didn't seem to make Mario nervous, but it certainly made his family impatient. It was clear there was no time to lose; his fighting spirit could only go so far before his disease would take over.

Finally, after a wait that felt like forever, it was time to get some answers. The appointment was at the Fiona Stanley Hospital in Perth at 9:00am. This meant a very early start, having to leave home before dawn. Mario and Maria picked up Suzanne on the way through. They greeted each other still sleepy-eyed, and then set off. Mario had packed a bag of clothes and toiletries; he was eager to have the operation and thought that the surgeon might want to keep him up there to admit him to hospital. He was hopeful this would happen, and had prepared himself for the fact he might not be coming home with Maria and Suzanne. As positive as he was, he knew that this was what needed to be done in order to fight his cancer.

They arrived in Perth when the workers were starting their day. Maria drove through the busy city traffic but still made it to the hospital with time to spare. Navigating their way through the large hospital, they found the area where they needed to be. Sitting in the waiting room, they watched doctors appear and disappear from the hallway, taking a patient with them each time. Finally, Mario's name was called and the trio walked in unison into the surgeon's office. The surgeon introduced himself and shook Mario's hand. He gestured for Mario and Maria to sit down on the two chairs opposite his desk. Suzanne sat behind them, opting to sit on the bed as there were no more chairs.

'So I have a request from your doctor in Bunbury, asking me to see you about an interesting problem.'

He spoke in a soft, kind voice, which put the family at ease. The surgeon spent some time asking Mario about his previous bowel cancer, then his subsequent liver cancer. He reviewed Mario's scans, explained what he was seeing, and informed them about the function of the liver and spleen. It wasn't until about fifteen minutes into the appointment that the surgeon revealed what he was thinking. His next sentence immediately changed the atmosphere in the room, filling three hopeful hearts with disappointment.

'Removing the spleen is not usually a very difficult procedure. But in this case it is actually very, very difficult. In fact, it is pretty dangerous. There's a chance you could bleed to death, Mario. I'm just being honest.'

Mario sat leaning forward, listening to the doctor in silence. Maria only managed a one-word reply, 'Really?' This wasn't what they were expecting at all. The surgeon explained in more detail.

'The blood vessels are normally very small around the spleen, apart from the main one, but in your case, they are very big, sausage-sized vessels...'

'Are you saying, Doctor, sorry to interrupt. Are you saying I can have chemotherapy or is it too difficult?' Mario asked.

'I don't think you can have surgery, Mario; I'll be honest with you. I'm very worried. The last thing I want to do is kill you from bleeding to death and that is a very real possibility. Your blood and platelet count is very low and surgically, for us, if you look at how badly you're bruising from your injections, if we had to operate on the inside, all the raw areas could bleed a lot and we could be in a very difficult situation.'

'Okay. So what do you…'

'I mean, I know you are stuck between a rock and a hard place. At the moment it's very hard for them to consider giving you chemo and I don't know how many other options they have up their sleeve.'

'This was the last option,' Suzanne said.

'It's just a very difficult situation and I really don't know what the right answer is,' the doctor said sympathetically.

'Why did they suggest surgery then?' Suzanne asked. That question held the disappointment at having their hopes raised, only to be crushed just like that.

'Because they are not surgeons. They don't understand the technical side, just as much as I don't understand the chemo side of things. I've tried to explain to your oncologist – and I think she understands – surgically, it could be very dangerous. The main issue is not the size of the spleen, but it's the blood clot that you had over twelve months ago and all the new vessels that developed around it because of back pressure. For us to do an operation, we need to free up the spleen off the diaphragm. The blood vessels are shared with your stomach. Those would be enlarged as well. And then there's the main one – all the blood vessels feed into the spleen through that. I've been involved in these situations in the past and it is very scary as all the blood vessels are very fragile and very enlarged.'

It was clear from this conversation that this was the end of the road. But Maria had to ask, even though she knew the answer.

'Are there any other options?'

The surgeon exhaled his breath, pausing for a few moments.

'Can the affected part of the liver be removed…or…?' Maria's voice trembled ever so slightly.

'Well, that's what I was wondering, whether that was

talked about. I don't do liver surgery. I could give one of my liver surgery colleagues a call. Look, if you can't have the chemo, whether they could treat… it's quite a big tumour in your liver, uh, but, whether the liver tumour can be treated some other way.'

'I've already asked about radiation but she said no…' Maria said.

'I just seem to remember when Dad was first diagnosed, they said liver surgery wasn't an option because they wouldn't be able to remove part of it,' added Suzanne.

The surgeon asked to look at Mario's first liver scan, when the tumour was first discovered. They all sat in silence while he looked at it.

'I think the liver lesion is a little bit more advanced than I appreciated. Like I said, I'm not a liver surgeon. This all got picked up because of the clot and the clot may have been a deal breaker for liver surgery anyway…I'll give my colleagues a call; it may be worthwhile.'

The surgeon picked up the phone, dialled and waited. No answer.

He tapped his pen on the desk, unsure what he could offer this family who so desperately wanted something to be done.

He continued, 'Yeah, it's a bit tricky. The only other thing about having the spleen removed, is we normally need to vaccinate you a couple weeks beforehand because, what the spleen does, it also filters all the bacteria. We've had patients die from infections going through the bloodstream because of the lack of spleen.'

Mario, who had been sitting quietly for some time, asked, 'If you remove the spleen, will the body adjust itself to infection then?'

'The infections I'm talking about are the severe infections that can go through your bloodstream. It's very rare these days but that is because we give you a triple vaccination.'

Mario had another question. 'And if you do remove the spleen, is there a good chance that the white cells will come up again?'

'That's what I don't know. There's no guarantee in any of this. Another reason why your blood count may be so low is because your liver is not working properly because of the blood clot.'

'So it might not even be from the spleen?' Suzanne asked.

'Yes, the spleen could just be enlarged as a symptom of it. There's no guarantee that removing the spleen will solve the problem. But I also understand your oncologist doesn't have a lot of other options.'

They had been in the surgeon's office for almost half an hour. They were now just going around in circles, with nothing being resolved. The surgeon sensed their helplessness, their desire to have been given different news. He spoke with sympathy in his voice, warm and gentle because he couldn't do much else for them.

'I'll need to get some blood tests today to see what's going on. It's all a little bit confusing at the moment. What I think we should do, I mean we're not going to resolve it today, but it's not something we can drag on for months. Obviously things are progressing. What I might do is get some blood tests today. I'll give you a script for some vaccinations to have in Bunbury. It won't do you any harm, even if we don't end up doing the operation. The vaccinations take three weeks for the body to start building up immunity. And what I am going to do is have a chat to one or two of my colleagues, get them to look at your films as well and decide whether we can gamble and go ahead and get the spleen out.'

'Is it worth taking the risk to do the surgery?' Mario asked.

'Ultimately, it's your body. You need to be mindful that none of this guarantees you anything. If there are any complications from the surgery, bleeding or anything else that happens, you could be stuck in hospital for weeks. That's going to delay your treatment even more.'

Maria got some papers out of her bag. 'Do you want to see his liver function results from yesterday?'

The surgeon took them and scanned his eyes over the numbers. 'Yeah, it's pretty bad. It has certainly changed a lot from October last year. I'll be honest…I don't have a good feeling about any of this in terms of surgery, I really don't. I've been in this situation before. We pin all our hopes on this one thing and if it doesn't go perfectly, if things go really bad, you look back and think you could have had some extra time rather than go through all this and suffer from complications. I'll be honest, it's a set of very scary figures…have you got an appointment with your oncologist at all?'

'No, she just told us to let her know when the surgery is going to be.'

'Yeah,' the surgeon replied, almost apologetically. 'I'll chat to my colleagues and I think we need to meet up again, maybe next week? Is that all right?'

'Yep,' Maria managed, tears in her eyes and a lump in her throat.

Suzanne asked, 'I don't know if you could answer this, but, because it is at an advanced stage, would having chemo even do anything?'

'Oh, we never give up hope but it's going to be a really difficult question as to how much chemo we can give your Dad, and whether it is going to translate to something meaningful.

The doctor turned to Mario. 'I'd like you to see your oncologist before you see me next week, just to ascertain if there are *any* other options that they could consider. Because, as I said, there are no guarantees and there is a risk you may be worse off. At the end of the day, the chemo won't make the cancer disappear. Understand that. Ultimately, the cancer is going to keep growing and chemotherapy is not going to cure you. In reality, you have to ask yourself whether all this is worth it. The surgery is very high risk and could leave you worse off than where you are now.'

'It's just hard because, when Dad had his brain bleed, they also said the same thing – it was high risk – and he came through...' Suzanne offered.

'But with that one, he had very little choice. Either have the surgery or the blood clot in his brain would have extended. That's a different sort of situation; it was literally life or death. There was very little to lose in that situation. If they didn't do anything, he would have died from the blood clot due to the brain expanding.'

The doctor looked to Mario. 'In this case, if I don't do anything, if you don't have any surgery, you'll find in two weeks' time, you are the same as what you are now.'

There was nothing more to discuss. They had spent just over forty minutes with the friendly, kind and honest doctor. He had been patient, knowing that the family was struggling to accept his answer.

'Thank you, Doctor,' Mario said, smiling as he walked out the door with his wife and daughter.

'I'll see you next week. Nice to meet you, Mario.'

Mario, Maria and Suzanne went to the reception desk and booked another appointment for the following week. With heavy hearts, they walked slowly out of the room and into the corridor.

'Dad, did you understand what the surgeon told us? How do you feel?'

'You know, if this is it, then I'm ready for Heaven. I've had a good life, have a wife and a beautiful family. I'm not giving up; I hope God saves me again. I've known people who have been worse and they survived. So I'm not giving up. But I am a number now. When God sets His sights on someone, you can't escape it.'

Suzanne had been trying hard to fight back the tears, but as Mario spoke, they spilled over. She quickly wiped them away, unsure of what to say. Mario had this amazing mix of acceptance and fight; he knew that what was happening was out of his control and his faith assured him of where he was going. Yet, he still had his fighting spirit, unwilling to give up on his life. He still had hope, even though the appointment they just had proved that there was no reason to hope for recovery.

There was a hospital cafeteria close by, so they decided to sit down and order some coffee and muffins.

While they drank and ate, Suzanne asked, 'Is there anything you want to do?'

'I want to get the downstairs room cleaned out. I feel guilty leaving jobs for Mum. I don't want to enjoy myself, I just want to get the jobs done so Mum doesn't have to do it.'

Maria and Suzanne, although touched by his selflessness, had other ideas.

'We don't mean that. Don't worry about jobs for now, just think about things you would like to do, experiences you would like to have.'

'Okay,' Mario said. 'I'll have a think about it.'

They spent the rest of the time talking about other things, trying to avoid thinking about the inevitable, sad truth that lay before them.

Mario was exhausted by the time they got back to Suzanne's. He went straight to the couch and it wasn't long before he was breathing peacefully. After a decent nap, he awoke. He looked at the clock and realised it was almost time for Jordan to return from work. He paced around, then said to Maria, 'I'm feeling uneasy, Darling.'

Maria and Suzanne exchanged glances, assuming he was referring to the appointment. Expecting a deep and meaningful comment, they waited for him to speak.

'I don't know whether to have a cup of tea now, or wait for Jordan…I'll do the polite thing and wait for Jordan.'

Maria and Suzanne laughed and then Mario laughed along too. Those kinds of comments were what made Mario unique; he had these quirky one-liners that he delivered with utter sincerity, his choice of words often made his family laugh.

Later that afternoon, Matthew and Stephanie came to Suzanne's, to discuss what the surgeon had said. The family sat in the front room; Maria and Suzanne took turns to relay what the surgeon had told them.

Matthew looked at Mario and asked him, 'How are you feeling about all of this, Dad?'

'I'm reflecting on today but taking it with a brave heart.'

Mario certainly had a brave heart; he sat calmly and spoke with ease, as if his family was discussing everyday matters, and not his terminal illness. One point of discussion was whether they should even go back to Perth and put Mario through the tiring trip, when the surgeon had made it pretty clear it was not a good idea to operate. They debated this for a while, and then came to the conclusion that they would take Mario back. He wasn't done with fighting, so they weren't either. He always had hope, so they would take him back to Perth, just in case there was a slight chance the surgeon had something different to offer.

Mario started looking tired, and everybody's stomachs were telling them that it was time for dinner, so they wrapped up the emotionally exhausting conversation.

Mario, with a smile and a very official tone of voice said, 'All right, let's close the family meeting.'

The family laughed. Again, Mario managed to make his family smile and lighten the mood, even when their hearts were aching for what they knew they were going to lose.

22

Quality Over Quantity

The next week and a half was filled with more appointments. Only a day after the consultation with the surgeon in Perth, Mario went back to see his oncologist. She had made it clear that there was nothing more she could do, but they went to see her to discuss what the surgeon had said and find out where to from here. Mario told her about his headaches so she ordered a CT of the head, as well as an ultrasound of the liver. She wanted to see if there were any blockages in the liver, because if there were, she could possibly organise for a stent to be put in to help drain any bile.

Before they left, Suzanne asked, 'Based on Dad's symptoms, and the fact that nothing can be done, how much time do you think he has left?'

'If things stay stable, then possibly six to twelve months. If things start getting worse, then possibly less than six months.'

Mario had the ultrasound of his liver on the 20th of March. The next day, Mario, Maria and Matthew went to Perth to see the surgeon. As expected, he had the same answer as the previous week. He had spoken to a team of surgeons and oncologists and they all shared the same view – surgery would be too risky and there would be no real benefit to putting Mario through the trauma of an operation that may reduce his life span even further.

'Right now,' the surgeon said, 'you can enjoy life. You can enjoy your meals; you can go out into the sunshine and spend time with your family. At the moment, the focus is on quality over quantity. The sad reality is that there will be an end point. No one knows when, we just have to watch and see how you progress.'

'I agree, Doctor,' Mario said. 'I think you have made the right decision.'

The doctor wished Mario all the best, and the three thanked him as they headed out the door. The kind, empathetic doctor who had been the bearer of bad news waved goodbye, knowing that he wouldn't see Mario again.

On the 22nd, the day after they went to Perth, Mario had the CT scan of his brain. He had still been experiencing headaches, and, at times, felt off balance when he was walking.

On the 27th, Mario went to see his oncologist for the results. She noticed that he was jaundiced but thankfully, the brain scan showed no signs of lesions or brain bleed. It didn't explain why Mario was off balance and getting headaches, but at least nothing sinister had been picked up. The ultrasound of the liver showed there wasn't a problem with any blocked ducts, so there was no need for a stent.

She checked Mario's blood test results and found that his markers had jumped up again, but his blood count had gone back within the normal range.

'Hmm, I don't know why that's happened. While your cell counts have now jumped up to a level where I could give chemo, my concern would be that it could make it worse, seeing as the liver function has become worse.'

'You can't win, can you?' Maria said.

'No. If this was a few weeks ago, I would have said let's get on and do it. But it could change again. I'll monitor your bloods and if they stay at a consistent level, we can relook at chemo, but we will have to wait and see. I suspect it won't stay up though.'

It was frustratingly ironic – when one issue seemed to have resolved, another issue was standing in the way of the possibility of more treatment.

Eyes downcast, Maria said, 'I don't know…it's just…it's just hard.'

'It is hard,' the oncologist acknowledged. 'What I might do, if you agree, is link you in with the palliative doctor.'

'What does she do?' Maria asked.

'She'll be able to help with symptoms if and when they develop.'

There wasn't much else the oncologist could do for Mario. They had exhausted their options; it was now a matter of wait and see. Again, Mario thanked her for looking after him. He had been her patient for over a year, just one of many, and now he was stepping out of another doctor's office, never to step foot in it again. Over the last month or so, he had been referred from doctor to doctor, in the hope that they could offer a way to extend his life. Each time there had been hope offered only for it to be replaced with disappointment. The time had come to stop focusing on possible 'what if' treatments, and start focusing on giving Mario some treasured memories in the short time he had left.

23

Making Memories with Mario

An Italian tradition that Mario's family had been doing for many years was to make their own tomato sauce. They would generally do it when the weather was warm and the tomatoes were ripe. Long ago, Mario had hand-made many of the utensils and equipment needed to make the sauce. He had made a large cooker, a set of burners, a big wooden spoon and a big wooden strainer. Normally, they would have preferred to do it in February, but this year, with everything that had been going on, they postponed it for a little while. They even debated whether they should even worry about doing it this year, but as Mario was still well enough, they figured they should. Mario might not get to be part of another tomato sauce making day, so they ordered the tomatoes, and the on the 31st of March, the family put on their old clothes and set to making the delicious sauce. It was a process that took all day – washing and sterilising bottles and washing the tomatoes in big, plastic bins filled with water. The tomatoes were cooked until they were soft, then transferred into a little machine that fed them through and turned them into sauce. The pulp was put through a couple of times, until the tomatoes were dry and drained of all their liquid. Next, the sauce was poured into the bottles and stacked into big drums filled with boiled water. The bottles cooked, steaming and bubbling away and filling the air with the aroma of tomatoes. It was a tiring procedure and one in which Mario couldn't participate. Most of the day, he sat on the verandah and watched, and every now and then when he felt strong enough, he would walk down to the shed to observe. Hands on hips, he would smile as he listened to and joined in with the family's conversations. He would offer advice if they needed it; he would supervise and tell them if he thought they could do it a better way. When his legs tired, he would walk back to his chair on the verandah, watching from afar again. That day, while watching his family do the work that he couldn't, he felt down. He was frustrated that his body felt so tired and weak. He had lost his willpower; he hated that all he could do was sit and watch, not being able to help. He didn't tell anyone he was feeling this way at the time, instead, when the sauce was finished, he smiled and thanked everyone for all their efforts. It wasn't until a couple of days later that he confided in Suzanne. That mood didn't last long, though, as he told Suzanne that afterwards, he had begun to feel better and stronger and he 'gained a new lease on life.' He had found his willpower again, and the positivity that he was so good at.

For all this positivity, deep down he knew that his future was limited. He didn't vocalise this, but sometimes, it weighed on his mind. He sat on his couch, smiling as he watched Emmy playing. He admired her young, carefree face and felt a pang deep in his heart. He wouldn't get to see that face change, her features merging into maturity as the years went by. She came close, and he reached out his arms and drew her in. Kissing her on her sweet-smelling head, he said to her, 'I'm going to watch down on you from Heaven.' Emmy smiled up at him, his words no cause for alarm for her young mind. She wriggled out of his grip and went back to playing.

The next day, Suzanne was talking to Emmy about her Nonno. Emmy looked at Suzanne, her little mind thoughtful.

'Nonno is so sick.'

Suzanne breathed deeply, then answered, 'Yes, darling, he is very sick. That's why he sleeps a lot.'

Emmy pondered this for a second. 'And the doctors can't fix him.'

Her answer made Suzanne's chest tighten. 'No, honey, they can't. That's why Mummy is sad sometimes. He won't get better.'

Suzanne looked at Emmy sadly, her eyes filling with a watery film. Emmy looked back at Suzanne, her big eyes yet to truly see the way the world works.

'You can get a new Nonno,' she suggested.

Fighting tears, Suzanne reached for Emmy. Softly, she said, 'No, honey, it doesn't work that way.'

And just like that, Emmy was off again, her attention on something else. Her innocence trailed behind her like a cape, protecting her from the troubles of life. Suzanne, on the other hand, sat still and pensive, the conversation sitting heavy on her heart.

*

It was time to start thinking about making special memories with Mario. Knowing that he loved Holden cars, Suzanne had the idea that they could find someone who owned an old Holden and see if they would be willing to take Mario for a drive in it. It so happened that Stephanie's boyfriend, Luke, was also a car enthusiast and he was able to get in contact with a man who lived in Busselton. Steve owned a Classic Holden Monaro GTS and he was willing to drive to Mario's house, pick him up and take him for a spin around Bunbury.

On the morning of Saturday the 8th of April, the family excitedly gathered at Mario and Maria's house. Mario thought that they had all come for a visit and greeted them happily. At 10:30am, a bright green Holden Monaro pulled into the driveway.

'Mario,' Maria called. 'Go outside, someone is here to see you.'

'Okay, Darling,' Mario said. He opened the front door and looked out. As soon as he spotted the car, his mouth widened into a huge smile and he started walking down the stairs.

'Oh, look at this!' he exclaimed, holding onto the rail as he tried to get to the bottom quickly. 'My favourite, a GTS! That's a beauty! Original!'

He eyed off the car as he walked towards the owner, smiling the whole time. Pointing at the car, he said, 'I didn't have a Monaro but I had a HQ.' In the same breath, Mario extended his hand. 'Hello, how are you? Pleased to meet you.' Having never met Steve before, Mario started talking to him as if they had known each other for years.

'I love the GTS and I wish I owned one. My HQ had twin headlights on the front. I did it myself. The only thing it was a 202, it didn't have a V8. Is yours a V8?'

'Yeah,' Steve answered, chuckling, and before he could say anymore, Mario was talking again.

'GTS would have come out with a V8, you know. Very nice. I even have a Holden shirt.' Mario pulled at his shirt, smiling at Steve and laughing.

'Would you like to go for a drive?' Steve asked.

'Yes please,' Mario answered without hesitating. Then added, 'Could we take a look at the engine first?'

Steve nodded and Mario lifted up the bonnet, excited to

see the mechanics of the car. 'Look at this!' he said admiringly, and proceeded to ask Steve more questions. When he had finished admiring the engine and all the parts, Mario instantly accepted Steve's offer to sit in the driver's seat. He was like a child in a candy shop, eyes wide with excitement. He couldn't wipe the smile from his face as he sat, gripping the wheel. He looked around, feeling the roof interior with his hand.

'All black interior. I love that.' His hands found the steering wheel again. 'Beautiful!'

He looked out the window, his wide smile evident for all to see. Perhaps as he sat there, in a motionless car that was not his own, he was taken back to a time when he was young and strong. Perhaps he was driving his Holden, the window down and the breeze ruffling his hair. He may have remembered what it was like to work on his own car with his own hands, and then drive it with pride. To others it was just a car, but to Mario, it was a vehicle that allowed him to be taken back to a time when he was healthy and fit, when he had his life ahead of him.

His nostalgia was interrupted when Steve asked, 'Shall we go for a drive now?'

Mario got out of the car and went around to the passenger side. Steve hopped in the driver's side, while Maria, Matthew and Suzanne squished themselves into the back. Luke and Stephanie were going to follow behind in their own car. The Holden came to life, reversing out of the driveway, the engine purring and then roaring as it gathered speed.

'Listen to that engine, Dad,' Matthew said.

Mario didn't answer. He had his arms folded across his stomach with a small smile on his face. It was the quietest he had been since he first saw the car parked in his driveway. Clearly, he was wrapped up in enjoying the experience.

Mario was driven around to the places that had some significance to him. They drove past the old power station, where he used to work. They drove up to the Cut, a rock wall lined channel linking the Leschenault Estuary to the Indian Ocean. It was located behind the inner port and was a favourite spot where they used to go for family drives on a Sunday after church. They slowly drove by his old house on Bolton Street.

Mario pointed out the window as they approached it. 'This one here. That's the one, Darling.'

'That's a nice little house,' Suzanne said.

The neat house was situated on one half of a large block of land, with a couple of steps leading onto a small verandah. The other half had numerous caravans parked on the neatly trimmed grass. The house had been restored.

'Is this where you grew up?' Steve asked.

Mario looked at Steve as he spoke. 'They knocked everything down and put caravans everywhere. That was our first home in Australia.'

After they finished taking a drive down memory lane, Steve drove them to a café overlooking the back beach. There they all enjoyed a coffee and when Steve rose to leave, Mario shook his hand. 'Thank you very much, I really loved it.'

The family also thanked Steve profusely, very appreciative that this kind man took time out of his day to help create a wonderful memory for Mario.

Luke and Stephanie drove them to another restaurant, one that was close by and also overlooked the beach. The rest of the family joined them and they enjoyed lunch together, soaking in the happiness they had brought Mario that morning.

A couple of weeks after Mario's car ride, the family surprised him again. He had expressed an interest in wanting to fly in a plane, as he had never before been on one. Luckily, Jordan still had the contact details of his real estate agent, Joel, who was also a qualified pilot and owned a six-seater aircraft. Joel very kindly agreed to make this experience happen for Mario and very generously said that he did not want any payment.

Although it wouldn't be the same as a large, commercial aeroplane, it was the best they could do. Mario had never been well enough or motivated enough to travel, so this small plane that would fly around Bunbury for a short period of time would suit just fine.

The plan was to meet Joel at the Bunbury airport at lunchtime. Jordan, Suzanne and Emmy arrived first, followed by Matthew. Next Maria drove into the carpark, with Mario in the passenger seat and Stephanie in the back. As soon as Mario realised where he was, he smiled and said, 'Darling, am I going for a plane ride?'

'Yep! Are you up for it?'

'Yes, Darling,' Mario replied. 'This is great!'

They got out of the car and went across to meet everyone.

'Hi, Dad,' Suzanne greeted him, giving him a hug. 'You ready to fly?'

'You nervous at all, Dad?' Matthew asked, swallowing some travel sickness tablets.

'No, I'm looking forward to it!'

After a little wait, Joel's car pulled into the carpark. He wound down his window and told the family to follow his car through the gates and into the hangar. Jordan introduced him to everyone, and Joel shook their hands and smiled. He was a confident, charismatic man, easily making conversation and jokes about flying. 'I hope you're feeling confident today, because I'm not,' he teased.

Once Joel had prepared the plane, it was time for the passengers to get in. It was a tricky entry, having to climb up onto the wing and get into the plane through the passenger door, which required bent knees and a hunched back to climb into the tight space. As the aeroplane was only small, Matthew, Stephanie and Maria would accompany Mario and Joel. Jordan, Suzanne and Emmy were the ground-based spectators, taking photos and videos of the whole affair.

Thankfully, it was a beautiful day, with only a light scattering of clouds in an otherwise blue sky. The plane roared to life and the propellers started turning. Joel got everyone to put headphones on so they could communicate over the noise of the engines. Then they taxied out to the runway and almost immediately started to accelerate for takeoff. Before long, they were airborne and Mario finally had the chance to view the world from up high. He was able to experience the flutter in his stomach as the plane went from solid ground into the air. He smiled as the ground moved further away and he had a bird's eye view of the beautiful landscape that lay beneath him. With arms folded in his lap, he took in the sight, marvelling at the world below. Joel flew around Bunbury, taking them over Mario and Maria's house. They continued out over Australind and then across the city centre and over the beach. Mario thought the view was beautiful – the great expanse of dark blue water and the light blue sky. The crooked lines where the water met the land. The wide-open spaces, interspersed with green bush, buildings and houses. The place that Mario had called home since he was ten years old sprawled before him. He loved seeing his home from a different angle, the way a bird would, soaring high and free.

They flew for about thirty minutes, Mario loving every moment. Mario could see the three excited figures waiting on the ground below and, as the plane landed, he waved and smiled at them. Joel steered the plane into the hangar, and Mario still wore a smile on his face.

'Thank you very much,' he said appreciatively to Joel.

'My pleasure!' Joel answered, turning off the engine.

Once everyone had alighted from the plane, Jordan and Suzanne bombarded them with questions. But the look on Mario's face said it all.

'It was fantastic! I'll cherish this forever,' he beamed. Another precious memory was stored away for Mario and his family, who were trying to fit as many in before it was too late.

Scan this QR code to watch a video of Mario's ride in the Holden Monaro.
Or visit:
www.suzifaed.com/holden-ride/

Scan this QR code to watch a video of Mario's flight over Bunbury.
Or visit:
www.suzifaed.com/bunbury-flight/

ABOVE: A family tradition of making Tomato Sauce, using the equipment Mario made by hand, 31st March, 2017.

ABOVE & RIGHT: Mario's surprise ride in a Holden, 8th April, 2017.

ABOVE: Mario's surprise flight around Bunbury, 19th April, 2017.

24

Another Hospital Visit

It was fortunate that Mario had the flight when he did. Only three days later, on the 22nd of April, he was admitted to Bunbury Hospital. In the previous weeks his feet had become swollen, as did his ankles. Then his family noticed his stomach had grown too.

A couple of days before being admitted to hospital, Mario and Maria had visited the Oncology unit. They wanted to give the nurses who had looked after him a thank you card and some flowers. The nurses immediately noticed his round, enlarged belly. Concerned, they rubbed his stomach.

One nurse said, 'Mario, your stomach is very swollen. It looks like you have fluid building up. The liver isn't filtering properly and so all the fluid causes your stomach to swell. If it gets really uncomfortable, I suggest you go to the Emergency Department and ask them to drain it.'

As it turned out, Mario did start to become rather uncomfortable. He could barely bend over, and because he was carrying extra weight, his legs were sore and it was difficult for him to stand. So, on the morning of the 22nd, Maria took Mario to the Emergency Department and explained what was happening. After an initial assessment it was determined that Mario should be admitted. Neither he nor Maria had been expecting that; they had thought the process would be simple and Mario would only need to be there for a couple of hours. As it was, he had to stay for five days. Having fluid drained is normally a simple procedure, but in this case, it was complicated and they had to approach with caution and complete the procedure slowly. Once he had been assigned a bed in the ward, the doctors set about organising an x-ray, blood tests and a CAT scan.

Being the weekend, it wasn't until the Monday that the doctor had a chance to examine the results and when he did, he found a very diseased, scarred, badly functioning liver, and a large amount of fluid buildup within the stomach. After assessing how much fluid was present and discussing the possible complications of the procedure, a long thin tube was inserted into Mario's side. It would remain there for the next few days, the nurses coming in every now and then to empty the yellow fluid that had pooled into the attached bag.

Despite this, Mario remained in high spirits, enjoying visits from his family. At one point, as Suzanne sat next to him, he looked at her and repeated his mantra.

'I'll keep fighting,' he reassured, then added, 'I hope I make it to see your first book published.'

'So do I, Dad,' Suzanne said softly, fighting back tears.

By the 27th, the doctors had filtered out almost ten litres of fluid and Mario's stomach was looking noticeably smaller. As he left the hospital, he felt relief. Moving easier, feeling lighter, he felt much more comfortable. His feet and ankles had returned to their normal size and his skin no longer had a yellow tinge. For now, even though his insides told a different story, on the outside Mario looked healthy and happy.

So it was, through his dogged determination and perseverance, Mario was blessed to see another birthday. His sixty-sixth was spent at home with Maria, Suzanne and

Emmy. After work, Jordan, Stephanie, Gina and Catena joined them and all enjoyed a tasty homemade lasagne, at Mario's request.

That weekend, after Mario had been resting on what was a lazy, quiet Sunday, family started arriving at his house.

'Darling, what's going on?' he asked Maria, as he looked out the window and saw their driveway looking like a car yard.

'I organised an afternoon tea for you.'

'Thank you, Darling. I was wondering why you've been busy cooking all that food!'

He went outside to meet his guests, greeting them all with big hugs and wide smiles. Both sides of the family were there, as well as their good friends Frank, Filomena, Ron, Brian and their wives. Mario was ecstatic to see that everyone had come for him. But there was one more surprise. There was one special lady missing at the party – Mario's sister, Josephine. Given that she too was unwell it would never have been expected for her to travel down to see him. Mario was in the laundry when he heard a knock on the door.

'Mario,' Maria called. She paused, and then knocked again.

'Yes,' he called back, wondering why he was being hurried along. When he opened the door he found Josephine standing there waiting for him.

Immediately, his face lit up and he beamed at her.

'Oh, Josephina! Hello! How are you? Good to see you!' They kissed each other on the cheek and embraced.

'Hello,' Josephine laughed as they held on tightly to each other while the family watched on with tears in their eyes.

The sibling's emotional reunion was both heart-warming and heart-wrenching to witness. The distance that had separated them for years, and the health problems that had prevented them from seeing each other more regularly did not erase the love they had for each other. For the rest of the afternoon and into the early evening, they sat side by side. As the sky darkened and the air cooled, everyone started to leave. Mario bade farewell to all hugging them as usual, but when it was time for Josephine to leave, he hugged her that little bit longer. Josephine cried openly as she got into the car.

'Goodbye, Josephine,' Mario said. 'We'll try and come and see you soon if I feel well.'

'Ciao, Mario,' Josephine sobbed.

As the car pulled out of the driveway and drove away, the brother and sister continued to wave. Josephine's tears and Mario's smiles testament to the power of their love since their earliest childhood days in Italy. It was the last time they would ever see each other.

Scan this QR code to watch a video of Mario's reunion with Josephine.
Or visit:
www.suzifaed.com/reunites-sister/

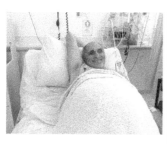
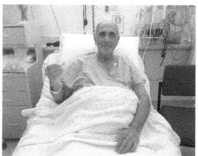

ABOVE LEFT: *Mario admitted to hospital full of fluid, Bunbury Regional Hospital, 22nd April, 2017.*

ABOVE RIGHT: *Noticeably smaller after having almost ten litres of fluid drained, 25th April, 2017.*

ABOVE: *Mario's surprise Afternoon Tea for his 66th birthday, back row from left – Armando, Wendy, Tony, Maria, Frank, Antoinette, Angie, front row from left – Connie, Josephine, Mario and Robbie, 7th May, 2017.*

25

Deterioration and Disaster

The following Friday, Jordan and Suzanne treated Mario and Maria to a weekend away. They had planned it as a surprise for them both; a combined present for Mario's birthday and a Mother's Day gift for Maria. All they had told them was to pack a bag and they would do the rest. When Jordan finished work, he met the others at Mario's house and an hour later they all arrived at their destination in Busselton.

'This looks nice,' Mario said, looking around at the façade of the luxury Broadwater Beach Resort.

Maria agreed. 'Very nice.' She followed him up to a two-story unit that overlooked tennis courts. By now the sun was setting and their stomachs were rumbling. Fish and chips were on the menu that night, and once Jordan and Suzanne put Emmy to bed, all the adults were able to relax. The scrabble board came out and as Maria, Suzanne and Jordan played, Mario sat and watched.

Suzanne glanced up now and then at her Dad and the look of quiet contentment almost broke her heart, yet in equal measure, gave her great solace.

The next morning, Mario awoke feeling lethargic. He was moving slower and talking softer. Somehow, it seemed, deterioration in his condition had taken place in the space of a night and he was to spend a lot of the day sleeping. While he slept, Maria, Jordan, Suzanne and Emmy explored the resort, and took Emmy for a swim. Jordan and Suzanne had a game of tennis and when Mario woke up, he slowly walked over to join them. The day passed all too quickly and once more, the scrabble board came out when Emmy went to bed. This time, Mario didn't join them at the table. He slept on the couch, one arm on the armrest, his head bent forward and his chin almost touching his chest.

The speed at which Mario had slowed down was incredible. Only the previous week he had been able to do some work in his shed and fix the bathroom taps at home. Now, he seemed to have withered. He walked slowly and was off balance at times. Seeing him decline noticeably over that surprise weekend brought the reality closer to home for the family. His smile was deceiving; for despite his external courage, inside his body was under enormous strain. His fighting spirit could only go so far, and it looked like the cancer was beginning to put up a strong fight too.

On the drive home from Busselton, they spent most of it in silence.

During the next week the deterioration became more evident. He was weaker, more tired and developed a sharp pain in his right side, no doubt caused by the pressure that his liver was under.

Suzanne sat with him one afternoon, both with cups of tea in front of them.

'Do you feel you are getting worse, Dad?' she asked.

Mario nodded. 'Yes. I'm still trying to keep positive but it's not working anymore.'

Tears welled up in Suzanne's eyes. No matter what, Mario had kept positive and refused to give up. Now, there was a hint of resignation in his voice. The unfairness of it all took Suzanne's breath away. There were no words that could make it better, no more discussion about the illness that could take it away. Instead, they just finished their cup of tea and talked about other things.

Mario mentioned again the work he wanted done around the house. There were two main jobs he wanted to complete. Although old, the house was still in good condition, but there were areas that had more wear and tear than others. One was the leaking shed roof that was getting worse over time. The other was the eaves all around the house – the paint had faded and was looking weathered, worn and badly in need of a fresh coat of paint.

The roof was the most pressing job. It was the original one from when Mario had built the shed and there were patches of rust everywhere. The previous winter, it had leaked from various places, water falling onto Mario's tools and workbench and cupboards. Buckets had been placed in the appropriate spots, but they couldn't leave it like that forever. Mario had received a couple of quotes from Tradesmen, but could not afford what was quoted. He was frustrated that he couldn't get it done, especially with the approach of winter. But, more importantly, he wanted to make sure the job would be done so that Maria would not be left to worry about it.

Suzanne could sense the frustration in his voice. She had heard him mention the shed's roof in the past. Driving home, she wondered how they could help fulfill Mario's wish to get his jobs completed and give him peace of mind.

On the Friday after Mario made that comment about his positivity not working anymore, his friend, Ron, came to visit. Ron was a jovial man who spoke loudly and loved telling stories of when he and Mario used to work together. They enjoyed each other's company, and Ron always made Mario laugh. But this time they talked about serious matters.

'How are you feeling, Mario?'

The pain in his side was not only still there, it had intensified and felt like someone was stabbing him.

Grimacing, Mario replied, 'Ron, I don't think I'll make it.'

'Hang in there, mate.' Ron tried to reassure his friend, who he could see was weakening before his eyes.

Later that day, Mario was still in pain, so Maria took him to the doctor. He prescribed some painkillers and that night at dinner, Mario took his first dose, hoping that they would relieve him of the stabbing pain in his side.

Over the weekend, Mario continued to take his painkillers. They had done the job – the pain in his side was much better. He awoke early on Monday morning, the 22nd of May. Maria was still asleep and he could hear Stephanie moving about getting ready for work. He sat at the kitchen table, eating his breakfast slowly. His head felt foggy, as though he was still half asleep. His limbs were heavy; he had to concentrate to navigate the spoon to his mouth. When his cereal bowl was empty, he reached for his Webster pack, which held the day's medications. He pressed the tab that said, *'Breakfast'* and his morning's medications fell into his open palm. He swallowed them all with a large gulp of water, then stood up and slowly made his way to the couch. He fell asleep quickly but didn't sleep for long. He woke in a daze, finding his head even foggier than before. He rose, and made his way back to the table. He picked up his Webster pack, pressed the tabs that said, *'Lunch'* and *'Dinner'* and watched the waterfall of tablets cascade into his palm. He had just swallowed them when Stephanie walked into the kitchen and saw him.

'Dad! What are you doing?'

Mario looked at Stephanie and tried to focus on her face. 'I…took my…tablets.'

Stephanie held up the Webster pack.

'Which ones did you take?'

Mario pointed to the 'Dinner' tab. But all three tabs had been opened and emptied.

'No,' she said, 'You've taken them all. You only needed to take the breakfast ones.'

'Oh, I…thought it…was…night time.'

'Come and sit down, Dad,' Stephanie said, and she helped him make his way back to the couch. She went and woke Maria, and as she was rubbing sleep from her eyes, Stephanie told her what had happened. Maria, still drowsy from sleep, took a moment for the information to sink in. Once it had, she got up and went into the lounge room. Mario was sleeping, his lips puckered as if waiting for a kiss. He inhaled and exhaled, his stomach rising and falling at each breath.

'I've got to go to work now, Mum, but let me know what happens. If things get worse, call me and I'll come straight back.'

'I will,' Maria answered. When Stephanie had left, Maria put her hand on Mario's arm and gently shook it.

'Mario,' she called, 'Are you all right?'

Mario's eyes fluttered open.

'Darling,' he mumbled. He fell back to sleep, clearly very drowsy. Maria called the Community Palliative Care and explained what had happened. The nurse advised that she had two options: either wait and see how Mario fared or take him to the Emergency Department. The nurse recommended the latter option and Maria agreed. It was best not to take any chances.

Luckily, Gina, Catena and Suzanne were coming over that morning to do some work in the garden, so Maria held off calling them as she knew they would be there soon. The phone rang and Maria picked up. Suzanne was calling ahead to ask if she could bring her dogs over, but when she heard her Mum answer in a flurry, she knew something was wrong. The question that Suzanne had intended to ask was forgotten, and a different one took its place.

'What's wrong? Has something happened?'

Maria spoke quickly. 'Your Dad was confused and took the whole day's tablets. I'm taking him to Emergency.'

Suzanne's heart skipped a beat. 'Wait for me, I'll come with you.'

Maria was helping Mario walk down to the car when Suzanne sped into the driveway. Gina and Catena were already there and helped get Emmy out of the car. Suzanne raced over and Mario gave her a dopey smile. He mumbled something, but couldn't make himself understood. He spoke like he was drunk. His words ran together and they couldn't make sense of what he was trying to say. He sounded like he did when he had the brain bleed. Could it be happening all over again?

Suzanne helped Maria get him into the car, then quickly went to Emmy to say goodbye. Emmy held her arms out, but Suzanne had to leave her with Gina as she hopped into the car. Confused, Emmy started crying. Gina tried to console her as the car backed out of the driveway. Their hearts pulled at the sight of Emmy sobbing, but their immediate concern needed to be with Mario. His head was bobbing back and forth; he was slurring then sleeping. The effects of the medication had well and truly taken hold, and Maria and Suzanne were beginning to get very worried. With Mario's liver already under significant stress, what would the added trauma do to his already failing body?

While Maria drove, Suzanne called Matthew to let him know what was happening, and messaged Stephanie to tell her that they ended up taking Mario to hospital.

On arriving they found a wheelchair for Mario, and as they pushed him through the doors of the Emergency Department, they silently prayed, *Please, don't let this be the way it ends*.

The triage nurse examined Mario and assessed his vital signs. She found them to be fine; thankfully, even though he was terribly drowsy, he could still understand what was going on around him. The nurse seemed to think it wasn't urgent, so they had to wait for a short while before the doctor called him in. It was the beginning of a long day, and having to wait for various results and answers. Maria and Suzanne sat next to Mario in the waiting room, watching him as he dozed. Every now and then he would wake, raise his head slowly and look around. He would mumble something; just sounds not words, and then would fall back to sleep again. He was asleep when the doctor called his name. Maria and Suzanne jumped up and smiled nervously at the doctor as he held the door open for them.

The doctor, with the help of a few nurses, transferred Mario from the wheelchair onto the bed. Maria recounted the events of the morning and the doctor made an educated guess that it was the painkillers that caused Mario's confusion. Maria confirmed that she had noticed Mario's brief lapses over the course of the weekend. Nothing that stood out too much, just subtle moments where he had asked something he should have known, or said something that didn't quite make sense. Not enough to cause alarm, but enough that it had obviously worsened overnight, culminating in him taking the wrong set of tablets.

Throughout the day, Mario had various tests – a blood test, a CT scan of the head, a chest x-ray and a urine sample. The urine sample proved to be the most difficult – it was hard to get Mario to pass urine when he was asleep most of the time. The nurse brought a bottle, asked Maria and Suzanne to step outside for a moment and attempted to wake Mario up. A couple of minutes later the door opened, and Maria and Suzanne saw that Mario was asleep and the bottle empty.

Keen to avoid recourse to a catheter, the nurse waited for a few minutes then repeated the procedure. This time, when the door opened, the nurse held the bottle up proudly.

The rest of the day passed slowly. Every now and then, Mario would wake up, and with all his effort, try to talk. Maria and Suzanne would lean towards him, listening intently and trying to piece together his mumbled words. Sometimes he was able to make himself understood.

He looked around the room. 'Where is Steph? Where is Luke?'

He looked at Maria and Suzanne. 'I feel sorry for you sitting there.'

He tried to readjust his position. 'You take for granted being able to move around.'

Finally, the test results were returned. All came back clear, but there was an elevated number that showed up in his bloods, indicating an infection somewhere. The doctors decided that Mario would stay overnight so they could monitor him. He was moved to the medical ward at St John's, right across from the nurses' station. Matthew and Stephanie came after work and joined Maria and Suzanne by Mario's bedside.

The sun was setting, and it wasn't long before the view of the courtyard was replaced with shadows. It had been a long day; the hours spent within the walls of the hospital had all blended into each other. The rattle of the crockery on the trolleys being pushed through the halls signalled it was dinnertime. The smell of the warm food drifted through the doors. At least Maria and her children knew they could eat a meal and satisfy their hungry bellies. She felt sorry for Mario, who hadn't eaten or drank anything all day. He was still too drowsy to do either and it was risky to try in case he choked.

As much as they all wanted to stay, Matthew had to get home to his family, and so did Suzanne. Maria would remain until the doctor came, so Stephanie waited with her for a while. Mario was oblivious to what was going on and had no concept of the time. He continued to sleep, waking intermittingly but never for long. Finally Maria left her sleeping husband, hoping she would see him in a much better state in the morning.

Fortunately, when Mario's family visited him the next day, they did find him in a better state. He had regained the ability to speak properly and was able to stay awake for longer periods. It was a relief to see him eating and drinking, refueling his exhausted body.

'You know how to keep us on our toes,' Suzanne joked, trying to make light of the stressful situation. 'Do you remember anything about what happened yesterday?'

Mario shook his head. 'No, it's all a blur.'

Maria and Suzanne filled him in, and even after hearing what happened, he couldn't recall anything. It was difficult to have an in-depth conversation with him as he was still feeling tired and weak, so for the most part they just sat beside him and kept him company.

Another day and night passed. Mario was still quite tired and spent most of the time sleeping. As he had stopped taking the painkillers that caused the problem in the first place, the pain in his right side had come back. For now, the only option was to take some Panadol, which seemed to make him more comfortable.

Suzanne came for a visit and not wanting to wake her Dad, who had nodded off again, she simply pulled a chair up to the bedside. When Mario opened his eyes, he saw his daughter smiling at him. He returned the smile and rubbed his eyes.

'Hello, Suzanne,' he greeted warmly.

'Hi, Dad. How are you feeling?'

Mario had been asked that question so many times over the duration of his cancer journey and the answer had always been much the same. He would smile and answer positively, even if he wasn't feeling great. He might acknowledge that he felt tired or weak but he would never elaborate or start complaining.

Now, he simply said, 'I feel different to last time. I can't explain it, but I'm not myself.'

They spent some time chatting, with pauses in between to give Mario a rest. At one point, when they were talking about Suzanne's upcoming debut picture book, Mario said, 'I can't wait for your book to come out.'

'I know, I'm getting impatient now. I want you to see it.'

Softly, Mario answered, 'I'll look down on you from Heaven.'

Suzanne's reply caught in her throat. 'I'd rather you look at me from here.'

Mario said nothing, but he gave Suzanne a bright smile, as if that would mask the pain they both felt.

Later that evening, the doctor stopped in during his rounds. He spoke mainly to Maria as Mario wasn't able to retain the details of the medical conversation. The doctor seemed to think that Mario didn't have an infection after all and thought that the particular marker in the blood tests was raised due to the cancer. They couldn't give Mario those painkillers again, so would need to find another option for his pain management. The doctor also reviewed the many other medications Mario was on. He no longer needed to take Diabex, the medication for his diabetes, and he had been surprised that Mario was still taking them because, with the condition of his liver, that medication should have been stopped already. Even though Mario still had diabetes, he didn't need a long term management plan. To hear that was disconcerting – the doctor obviously knew the state Mario was in and couldn't envisage him being around much longer.

On the 26th of May, Mario was released from hospital. After days of doing nothing but lying in bed, he was lethargic and weak. But he was excited to be going home and leaving the confined space of the impersonal room. Mario and Maria were sick of the sight of hospitals; they had spent far too much time in them. Everything was uncertain and they didn't know if they would be back there again soon. There were signs that Mario's cancer journey was progressing. Powerless to stop it, all they could do was put one foot in front of the other and keep going. They would wait and see what each new day brought.

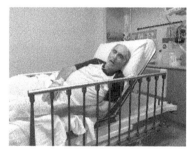

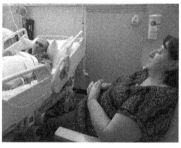

TOP LEFT: At the Broadwater Beach Resort in Busselton, showing signs of increasing tiredness, 12th May, 2017.

TOP RIGHT: Ready to check-out, from left – Jordan, Emmy, Maria, Suzanne and Mario, 14th May, 2017.

ABOVE LEFT: Back in hospital after an over-dose, Bunbury Regional Hospital, 22nd May, 2017.

ABOVE RIGHT: A picture that sums up many years of Mario and Maria's married life, St John of God Hospital, 24th May, 2017.

26

Surprises

Not long after Mario's hospital visit, Stephanie received a letter from Genetic Services. Back in April she had finally decided to have the test to determine whether she carried the BRCA1 gene. Some time had passed since Suzanne had tested negative; a result that had left it unclear whether Mario carried the gene or not. Given that one daughter had tested negative, the family hoped it was because Mario was not a carrier. Until they found out otherwise, they could still imagine that the family couldn't possibly have another health issue to deal with. Unfortunately, the letter revealed that Stephanie tested positive for the faulty gene. Genetics is like a lucky, or in this case, unlucky dip. Good and bad genes get passed on and there is no way to pick and choose. One gets what one is given. So there were mixed feelings in the family as they came to terms with the facts.

Once the shock wore off, they were able to consider the positive that came out of a negative situation. Sadly, it was too late for Mario, but Stephanie had time; she was still young. She was equipped with knowledge and could take steps to remain cautious and have checkups. If or when the time came, there were preventative measures she could take.

Having a positive result didn't mean she *had* cancer, it just meant she was at an increased risk of *getting* it. So, at this time, they didn't dwell on it. They needed to get over one hurdle at a time, and right now, the hurdle was honouring Mario's fight and being alongside him every step of the way.

Mario had been home for almost three weeks when he received some news from Suzanne that lifted his spirits. It was a Thursday afternoon, and he, Maria, Suzanne and Jordan sat around the table finishing off cups of tea.

Suzanne waited for a pause in conversation so she could surprise her Dad with news that would make him smile.

'So, Dad, I was thinking about your shed.'

Mario nodded. 'Yes,' he acknowledged, arms crossed and eyes focused on Suzanne.

'How are you guys going to come up with the money to get it done?'

As if truly perplexed by the question, he shrugged his shoulders and closed his eyes as he tilted his head into his shoulder. 'Just play it by ear, Suzanne.'

'It needs doing, doesn't it?'

Mario nodded again. He wondered where this conversation was leading.

'What if I told you that we have come up with the money and we are getting it done for you on Saturday?'

While Suzanne was speaking, Mario's mouth hung open as what she was saying sunk in. He paused for a moment and then broke into the smile she had known would come.

'Really? Where did you get the money from?' Excitement laced his question, his eyes lit up, shining.

'We've started a campaign, and all our family and friends have donated.'

His mouth widened again, the joy on his face evident. He opened his arms, inviting Suzanne for a hug.

'Oh, that's great, Suzanne! I really appreciate it. Thank you!'

'You'll get it done!' she said, as Mario hugged her tightly.

Moving back to her seat, she blinked away the tears that threatened to spill over.

'How much have you raised?'

'We've got $4,500 for you.'

'That's too much,' Mario said, not wanting to take anymore than was needed. 'The quote the blokes gave me was $3,000.'

'Well, what we've done is, we've got Struan and Gus…Gus used to be a roof installer. So they're coming on Saturday. Jordan and Matthew too. And we're going to get it done for you.'

Mario's smile almost reached his ears. He brought his hands together and raised them like he was praying.

'Oh, thank you so much! God bless you, Suzanne. Oh, thank you, another worry out the way.'

'That's it,' Suzanne replied.

'And you don't want the money back?'

'No, this is all for you guys. And with the left over, we'll maybe do the eaves.'

'Oh, that's great, thank you,' Mario said again, clasping his hands together. 'I really appreciate it.'

'That's okay. There have been a lot of family and friends who have donated so they have been very generous.'

'Oh, thank you very much. I'm really proud of you, Suzanne.' The joyful look on Mario's face remained. He beamed at his daughter, love and happiness radiating from his face.

Suzanne gave a bashful laugh. 'That's okay. I knew how badly you wanted it done. It's been a combined effort; everybody's chipped in.'

'I didn't want the shed getting ruined. The shelving and all that.'

'No, I know how much your shed means to you.'

'But family is first, though, you know,' Mario said, nodding and raising his hand towards Suzanne.

'Yeah. But you can rest easy now; it's going to be done.'

'So they've measured the sheeting and everything?' Mario asked.

'Yep. Gus, Struan and Matthew, they came and measured it all up when you were out. They've ordered two downpipes.'

'Lovely,' Mario said, nodding enthusiastically. 'So they are going to do the downpipes as well?'

'As well, yep.'

'Thank you so much!'

'That's okay. I was so excited to tell you.'

'Oh, that's good.'

'So, on Saturday, it will all be done.'

'This Saturday?'

'Yep, this Saturday.'

After that news, it was hard for Mario to wipe the smile from his face. He never asked for anything; didn't expect anything from anyone. But he was blown away by the generosity and was thrilled that, through the kindness of others, his shed could finally get fixed. A weight had been lifted from his shoulders. Afterwards, Mario and Suzanne were relaxing in the lounge room. The TV was on, Emmy was playing around them, and Maria was cooking dinner. There was a moment, shared only by father and daughter. That special moment, caught despite the noise that was going on around them. Suzanne looked over at Mario and caught his eye. He beamed at his daughter, giving her another wide and brilliant smile. She smiled back, and he mouthed the words, *'I love you.'* And just like that, the moment passed, but just as quick, it had settled itself in their hearts and there they could keep it forever.

Two days later, on the 17th of June, Mario woke early, excited that today was the day his beloved shed was getting fixed. It had been winter for two weeks and already they had received some rainfall. Thankfully, there were no rainclouds in sight; just the right amount of fluffy white clouds, a cool breeze and sunshine. After Mario finished his breakfast, he went out on the verandah and sat and waited for the workers to arrive. The materials had been delivered the day before, so when Struan, Gus and Jordan arrived, they were ready to begin work. Matthew was coming later, but thankfully Luke was down for the weekend, so they had another set of hands until then.

First, they drilled out all the bolts that held the rusty metal sheets to the roof. Mario stood next to the shed, with his hands on his hips and head raised skywards, watching the beginnings of the makeover. After resigning himself to the fact that he may not have been able to get the shed fixed, he couldn't believe that, just like that, it was happening. He felt very blessed. He was also tired, so he went back to his spot on the verandah and watched from there. He hated that he couldn't help but, as he watched the men pulling down the sheets and replacing them with new ones, he saw an image of his younger self. He thought back thirty-three years, to when, as a healthy young man, he had built his shed. Now, watching them bending and lifting and climbing, he saw himself completing those actions, the strength of his youth allowing him to work from dawn till dusk. That wasn't to be anymore, it hadn't been for a long time, but he still took delight in watching other hands fix something that had been made with his *own* hands.

It took the whole day to replace Mario's roof. Struan and Gus left mid-afternoon, when most of the work was done. Matthew and Jordan stayed to finish off, and, by 5:00pm, the only thing left to do was to install the new downpipes. That was a job that would have to wait for another day. The most important job was done. The sheets were shiny, the bolts weren't rusty, and hopefully, the new roof would last as long as the first one had. It was a shame Mario couldn't climb up the ladder to take a look, but Suzanne took some photos and showed him.

Mario smiled broadly. 'Ah, lovely. Thank you so much.'

He went to bed extra happy that night, knowing that there were so many kind hearts who cared about him enough to make his wish come true.

Scan this QR code to watch a video of
Mario being told about his shed.
Or visit:
www.suzifaed.com/shed-surprise/

Scan this QR code to watch a video of
making the shed dream a reality.
Or visit:
www.suzifaed.com/fixing-shed/

TOP: *Mario looks on as the work begins, 17th June, 2017.*

ABOVE: *The new roof being installed, from left –*
Gus, Luke, Matthew and Struan.

TOP: *Mario offering some advice from below, from left –*
Matthew, Jordan, Stephanie and Mario.

ABOVE: The new shiny roof.

27

Nearing the End of the Road

The next month passed by and as it did, Mario's symptoms returned. He had been getting progressively tireder, even more so than before. His feet began to swell again and his skin became yellow and itchy. He had also started to complain about having stomach aches. When he had last seen the doctor, his blood test showed his markers were still increasing, and were now 323. With such a big increase, the doctor thought it best to have another CAT scan. Mario had the scan and a blood test on the 18th of July. He had another appointment booked with the doctor for the following week, to get his results. However, later that same afternoon the doctor pre-empted the follow-up appointment and asked the family to come in the very next day. Maria played down the fear she felt and after a restless night, she dutifully led Mario and Suzanne back to the doctor's office. They were met with a sympathetic smile.

'I'm sorry to be the bearer of bad news, but I called you in earlier because I'm concerned things are progressing.'

She paused, letting the news settle, like an unwelcome visitor. The doctor continued. 'Mario, the cancer in your liver is more pronounced than seen in your previous scan. Your markers have doubled in just over a month – they are now 606. Your bilirubin is very high and your liver function is not good.'

The dreaded moment that they knew would come was finally here. Yet, it still felt unreal. As always, though, Mario kept himself calm and composed. He was even able to look across at his wife and daughter and smile. They sat tight-lipped, doing their best to keep composed.

Maria took a breath and asked, 'The fluid has obviously come back. I noticed his stomach, feet and ankles are even more swollen than yesterday. Can we get it drained again? Will that help things?'

The doctor shook her head. 'I'm not keen on draining the fluid again due to Mario's poor liver function. If it becomes very uncomfortable, I will, but I don't suggest it. His liver function is dramatically worse than last time so I think it would be too risky.'

With nothing left to offer, the doctor asked Mario what arrangements he wanted for his end of life.

'I want to die at home, Doctor,' Mario said. He had wanted that from the time he first found out that death was approaching.

'Okay, Mario,' the doctor replied. 'We can make that happen for you. I'll organise for the palliative nurses to visit every day. They can help set up a video conference with me when you are unable to come here to see me.'

She looked to Maria. 'Are you okay with having Mario at home until the end?'

Maria paused. She looked at Mario. Nodded her head. 'This is what Mario wants, so that's what we will do.'

'You know, the other option is hospital, where there is round-the-clock care. Often it can be a burden on families when patients die at home. But if this is what you want, then that's completely fine. I think it is very good of you to do this for Mario.'

Tears welled up, unspoken pain evident in Maria's eyes. 'It's the least I can do.'

'We'll still keep your appointment for next week and see where you're at. I'll get you to have another blood test before you come in. I'm sorry I didn't have good news for you.'

Mario got up slowly and smiled. 'Thank you, Doctor.'

She smiled back, aware of the devastation that her news had brought. 'Look after yourselves,' she offered. 'See you next week.'

Despite all that had occurred, the news was still hard to believe. That week between appointments went by as normal, Mario still smiling and keeping positive. Apart from his increasing tiredness and obvious jaundice, he appeared in good spirits. Of course, he moved slower, his actions were more deliberate and pronounced, taking more effort than normal. But other than that, he appeared well. He certainly didn't look like a person who was dying. Mario respected his doctor but he didn't want to believe what she said. She was going by the results of the blood tests, but she didn't know him. She didn't know the strength of his fighting spirit. He had had his low days, where he thought he might not make it. But to him, this was another hurdle to overcome, another challenge to rise up against and conquer. Even though his physical strength was diminishing, little bit by little bit, his mental strength was resilient. For his family, it was difficult to imagine that they were almost at the end of the road. How could it be real when Mario was calm and happy, still chatty and interested and enthusiastic? It was like they were standing on the shore, waiting for a massive wave to swell and crash. Watching the pull of the water as it forcefully dragged the sea into its grip. Holding their breath as the wave came into view, a tower of destruction rushing towards them.

Powerless bystanders, waiting for the impact; for only then would it become real. Only as the wave sweeps over them with its devastating power, will they realise that no amount of wishing it away will stop it.

So the week went on, and on Sunday, Mario and Maria had lunch with Matthew and Abbey. They enjoyed time with their grandchildren. After lunch, of which Mario had very little, he lay down on the couch and slept. Coby, who had been playing, looked over at his sleeping Nonno. He went to Maria and with innocent truthfulness, he said, 'Nonna, Nonno has cancer and that means he won't be in this world much longer.' Four years old, yet he could see and phrase what all the adults didn't want to believe.

Mario had his routine blood test, and the following day, the 25th of July, they braced themselves for the results. It had been a rush to get Mario to his appointment. Everything took longer now and so they were late. Normally on time, this was another sign that things were fraying around the edges, a rope almost at snapping point. The doctor welcomed them inside and Mario, Maria and Suzanne took a seat. While Suzanne set Emmy up on the floor with some toys, the doctor asked how Mario was feeling.

'Not too bad, Doctor. I've been tired and weak, but other than that, I'm okay.'

'Right. And what about any discomfort from the fluid build-up?'

'Not really. I'm still itchy but I'm not uncomfortable.'

'That's good,' she replied, raising her eyebrows in surprise.

Waiting for a pause in the conversation, Maria asked the dreaded question. 'So about Mario's blood tests. What did they show?'

The doctor's face softened, sympathy shadowing her eyes.

'I'm afraid things are worse than last week. Your liver function has deteriorated even further. The worry is that now toxins aren't draining because the cancer in your liver is blocking them.'

Mario leaned forward, his arms resting on his legs, hands clasped together. He smiled as he watched Emmy colouring in. No matter the news Mario received, he always remained relaxed. When this would be the time where most people would break down and sob, he sat calmly, as if oblivious to the implications.

His wife and daughter were doing their best to keep it together. This was becoming a regular experience for them; they had become well trained in keeping their emotions in check whilst sitting in a doctor's office, surrounded by the reality that was upon them.

The atmosphere in the room became heavy, as if the heartache felt was being transmitted into the air, suffocating the oxygen needed to breathe.

Fighting the lump in her throat, Suzanne found her voice and asked, 'I know it is hard to give an answer, but based on the results you've seen, how much longer do you think Dad has?'

The doctor paused, looking at the three faces in front of her. She turned to Mario.

'Do you want to know?'

Mario nodded his head.

'I'd say…based on what the results show…we are looking at weeks to months.'

'Okay, Doctor,' Mario said softly.

'Really?' Maria said, shocked at how little time he had left.

Suzanne shook her head. 'I can't believe it. I mean, I know what he has, but he *seems* okay. How can he be sitting here, looking fine, and not have long left?'

'I know,' the doctor said, compassionately. 'It happens very quickly. They can seem fine one day, and the next, become really sleepy then go unconscious. I'm so sorry; I don't want to be the voice of doom but I am telling you how it is. Hopefully, Mario will prove me wrong.'

Once again, Mario smiled at the doctor. She advised him to book another appointment for two weeks' time and again, she would check his blood test results before he returned.

Mario walked out of the doctor's office and into the hallway, Suzanne and Emmy on one side of him, Maria on the other. As Mario kept moving forward, he briefly lost his balance, wobbly on his feet. Maria and Suzanne put their hands out, ready to help him, but just as quickly as he lost his balance, he regained it. They laughed it off, Suzanne saying, 'Have you been drinking?' Laughing eased the tension, because they didn't want to admit, even after the prognosis, that the momentary stumble was indeed proof that Mario was losing his battle against the disease.

It wasn't long after that appointment that the doctor's words rang true. The family had been planning to take Mario away for a weekend. Abbey had found a beautiful little getaway in Pemberton, deep in Australia's southwest corner; ideal for relaxing and spending quality time together as a family. Mario had been looking forward to it, but unfortunately, as the time drew closer to the weekend, it was clear they wouldn't be able to go. There would be no more family trips that involved Mario. As the month of August began, he became considerably weaker, and spent most of his days either resting or sleeping on the couch. On the 2nd of August, one of the nurses from the Community Palliative Care team visited. Maria and Mario updated her on the latest news, both aware that they would be seeing the nurses a lot more. Where once they would visit sporadically, now they would become a more permanent fixture in their lives. Having been informed about Mario's condition, the nurse told them that she would bring a hospital bed next week.

'It may happen that one day you will be up walking around and the next you won't be able to get up, so it is good to be organised and ready for when that day comes.'

They spent over an hour discussing things; how Mario felt, how Maria felt, what to expect and the stages of grief. The nurse was impressed with Mario's attitude, the way he could still smile and stay positive. Before she left, she told him, 'You are amazing. A lot of people in your position would have died long ago. It is your positivity and mental strength that has helped keep you going.'

Even though Mario was not well enough to go away, he was able to enjoy some quality time with Matthew. On Saturday the 5th of August, Matthew came to the house. Mario greeted him with a hug and a smile.

'How are you feeling, Dad? You ready to come out with me?'

'Yes. I'm feeling weak but I won't let that stop me. I'm looking forward to it!'

Mario slowly shuffled along, unsteady on his feet and swaying slightly. Matthew walked closely beside him, always watchful for his father. When they got to the car, Matthew had to help him into the passenger seat.

They drove past the old house on Beach Road and along Ocean Drive, enjoying the view of the back beach, chatting as they travelled along. They arrived at the Backbeach Café and were seated next to the window, overlooking the ocean.

Mario smiled widely when his meal was delivered. He looked down at his full plate of fish, chips and salad, and his cappuccino.

'Lovely,' he said. 'Bon Appétit!'

He was not eating large meals anymore but that day, sharing time and conversation with his son, he ate slowly, enjoying every mouthful. As the café buzzed with the mingled chatter of the diners, Mario and Matthew enjoyed their own, private exchange. Their conversation flowed naturally and they talked about a variety of things – family, Matthew's work, Mario's working life, and memories. They talked about how Mario was feeling physically and emotionally. Despite Mario's body failing him, he still remained mentally strong.

As Mario finished off the last few bites from his plate, Matthew said, 'I'm proud of the way you have handled your sickness. I want you to know that I admire your strength and positive attitude.'

'Thank you, Matthew. And thank you very much for taking me out for lunch. I really loved it.'

'That's okay, Dad. I've loved having this time with you.'

They left with empty plates and full bellies and made their way out to the car. Matthew held onto Mario's arm as they walked past some outside tables. Mario's foot caught the edge of a table and he fell forward. His heart skipped a beat as the concrete path inched closer. His mind barely had time to process what was happening.

'Dad!' Matthew called out in alarm. Thankfully, he reacted quickly enough to catch Mario on the way down. They stared, wide-eyed at each other, before Mario regained his footing and exhaled deeply.

'Oh my goodness, Dad. You gave me a fright.' Matthew also exhaled in a sigh.

'Thanks for catching me.'

Mario looked down at the hard concrete. They both knew that they had just avoided a near miss. That their wonderful lunch could have been ruined by a moment that, thankfully, never came to be.

That special outing, shared between father and son,

turned out to be a fairly significant one. It was the last time that Mario would leave the house, besides from his upcoming doctor's appointment. Never again would Mario see the beauty of Bunbury. There would be no more drives with his family, no more cafés and conversation overlooking natural backdrops. From now on, for the rest of Mario's time, he would be confined. His freedom, precious and sacred, had become like an echo lost on the wind.

Like a deck of cards, so long precariously balanced and held up only by the player's tenacity and will, it was time for things to come crashing down. It was the 8th of August, and Mario had to see his doctor again. The difference in Mario's health from the last appointment was unbelievable. It had happened before his family's eyes, and yet, they couldn't believe the stealth and speed with which his cancer had snuck up and overpowered him. At each rise and fall of the sun, it seemed some more of Mario's strength left his body. Moving was strenuous, it took concentration and effort for Mario's limbs to do what he wanted them to. Because of this, he had started to use a walking frame. As much as he didn't want to rely on this aide, it was unavoidable now. Mario was losing something he prided himself on – his independence. Only the night before, he had to put his pride aside and ask Maria to help him dress for bed. Now, trying to get ready for his appointment, he needed help again. He sat on the edge of the bed, feeling like a child again, while Maria bent over, red-faced, putting his shoes on for him. As if matters weren't bad enough, Maria was unwell too. She had developed a nasty cough, and was clearly feverish and flustered.

Mario turned when Suzanne came in. If he was embarrassed about having his daughter see him needing help getting dressed, he didn't show it. Suzanne took over, bending down to put his other shoe on, while Maria went to get herself ready, coughing her way to the bathroom.

Suzanne helped Mario get down to the car. She stood beside him as he slowly put one foot in front of the other, steadying himself with the walker.

'How are you, Dad?'

'Good,' he replied. Then a little more honestly, but in his typically positive nature, never complaining for long, added, 'What a life…never mind.'

'I have to be honest,' the doctor said apologetically. 'I think we are on the downhill slide now.'

Mario entered the room in a wheelchair; they had left the walker at home and there was no way he would make it to the doctor's office on his own. Not that long ago it was an easy walk. Now it had become something out of reach, unfathomable that he could possibly make it there without help.

'How long?' Suzanne asked.

'We're looking at a week or two now.'

The heaviness in the room was back. It pressed down, forcing the air out of lungs. Tears could no longer be contained, and as Mario sat still, Maria and Suzanne cried for him. The doctor passed a tissue to each of them, gave them a moment for the news to sink in. Emmy, who had been playing on the floor, looked up.

'Mummy, why are you crying?'

Suzanne scooped her up and put her on her lap. Maria, feeling sick already, tried to stifle her simultaneous coughing and crying.

After a considerate pause, the doctor explained what would happen from this point. Some of Mario's medication would be stopped: his Clexane, because his blood wasn't clotting properly anymore. His fluid tablets, because they were no longer effective. Along with a list of new medications, the kind that one only needs when their body is in pain from dying.

'Mario, we'll set up a phone conference next week when the Palliative nurse comes to visit you. I think from now on, it will be too hard for you to come here. I'm sorry I can't do much more for you.'

Mario looked at the woman who had delivered the news of his life sentence. He looked at her and smiled.

'Thank you, Doctor,' he said sincerely and appreciatively.

The doctor laughed at her genuine and gentle patient. 'Oh Mario, you beautiful man. I could just wrap you up and take you home!'

And on that cheerier note to what was otherwise a depressing visit, Mario waved goodbye as he was wheeled out. Once again, leaving another doctor's office that he would never re-enter.

The oncology ward, where Mario and Maria had spent many hours over the last eighteen months, was just along the corridor. They decided to go and see the nurses there, one last time. It felt strange going back. Seeing the chairs where Mario had sat and the machines that had pumped the drugs through his system. Being surrounded by people acutely aware of their fragile mortality, the uncertainty evident in their eyes. It was a place where you couldn't help but think of death, but where there was still so much hope. Patients putting themselves through grueling rounds of chemotherapy so they could remain in this world for a little longer. Patients who came through the door were fighting their own battle. Some would win, some would lose. When the nurses saw Mario being pushed in a wheelchair, and the looks on the faces of his wife and daughter, they knew Mario's battle was close to being lost.

Those kind nurses are surrounded by people coming in and out their lives continuously. They create relationships with people they know they may never see again. They are used to a workplace where death lurks around each corner. But they brighten up the place; their laughter and cheery smiles make the patients feel more at ease. As much as Mario didn't enjoy coming to hospital every week, he had always looked forward to seeing the smiling faces of the kind nurses. Over the time he was a patient, the nurses had come to know and love Mario. His gentle nature, his positivity and patience had won them over, and he had appreciated the same qualities in them.

Four of the nurses, who had at one time or another looked after him, came to say hello. They approached the family with wide smiles, but with sadness in their eyes. They knew that Mario was here to say goodbye.

'Hi Mario!' they all said, as each of them bent to hug him.

'Hello, ladies,' Mario said, greeting them with his trademark smile.

Maria and Suzanne were already in tears, their quest to keep this reunion happy already failing.

Kerry embraced Maria. The nurse with a sparkle always in her eyes and a spring in her step was gentle and encouraging. She had a cheeky sense of humour and used it on many occasions to brighten the mood.

'He doesn't have long,' Maria whispered.

'Keep strong for the next part of this journey,' Kerry encouraged, rubbing Maria's shoulders.

While Maria and Suzanne dried their tears and put their pain on hold, the nurses bantered with Mario, as they always used to do.

'Look at you, Mario, getting pushed around, you lucky thing.'

Mario's belly rose up and down as he chuckled heartily. It

didn't take much to make Mario laugh; it came easily and frequently.

'We wanted to come to see you and say thanks again. Mario is very fond of you all,' Maria said, her voice breaking.

'Glad you stopped by. It has been good to see you again,' Kerry answered. Then added with a twinkle in her eye, 'So, Mario, who is your favourite?'

The nurses stood in front of him, in a line. Kerry. Nell. Debbie. Helen. They all smiled, waiting for his verdict.

Mario, having always been an honest man, replied, 'All of you...but Kerry is my favourite.'

They all laughed, which made Mario laugh again. Sometimes, when hearts are hurting, the best thing to do is laugh. Sometimes, when hearts are breaking, laughing is the only way to cope.

Surprisingly, Mario asked to have lunch at the hospital café after saying goodbye to the nurses. He ordered some chips, a favourite choice when they had done this in the past following his medical appointments. After the waitress delivered the plate of steaming chips, Mario looked at them then said, 'I don't mean to be morbid but these could be my last chips here.'

Morbid or not, sadly he was right.

As Suzanne and her Dad waited for Maria to bring the car close to the hospital entrance, they chatted.

'I'm sorry I made you cry before,' Mario apologised, as if her crying was his fault. 'Try not to worry; it'll make it worse. Be strong, like me.'

'I'll try, Dad, but I'm not as strong as you.' She paused, then added, 'Aren't you angry? You were so determined to beat this and now that won't happen.'

Mario shook his head. 'I'm not angry. My body is getting weaker but it makes me want to fight more.'

199

Over his lifetime, Mario had spent a huge amount of hours inside hospitals. Whether for his mental illness or his cancer, he had multiple volumes of thick medical records. Many times he had overcome the odds within their sanitised walls. Many times he entered sick, either fighting for his mind or body. Every time he was discharged, his fight successful. Except for this time. For on that cold and windy day, it was the very last time he would step into a place that had given him more chances at life.

ABOVE: Mario spends time with Coby, Matthew and Jesaia, 23rd July, 2017.

RIGHT: Mario's last special outing at the Backbeach Café, where he was able to enjoy a full meal, 5th August, 2017.

BELOW: Mario visits the nurses who cared for him during his treatment, St John of God Oncology Ward. From left – Kerry, Nell, Debbie and Helen.

28

The Final Fight

That last doctor's meeting seemed to signal the beginning of the end. As if by uttering the words, it set in motion Mario's descent. Over the past months, it had begun, barely noticeable. Slowly at first, incrementally, it started picking up pace and gathering speed; now the signs couldn't be denied. Mario's constant smiling face gave the family a false sense of security. Surely he would be okay; no one smiles like that when they are near death's door. His cancer had been creeping up, hiding behind the brightness of that smile. It had them fooled and so, when it was upon them, even though it had all been leading to this moment, it felt rushed and frantic. How could it have overtaken him so quickly? How could he be walking around one minute, eating regular meals, then end up housebound, too tired to move?

Time was running out; the countdown was on.

<u>9th August:</u>
Mario had taken up a semi-permanent spot on his couch. Too tired and weak, he couldn't do much more than sit or sleep. When he needed to go to the toilet, or have a bite to eat, he would slowly push himself up and use the walker to

get around.

One of the nurses from Community Palliative Care came and informed Mario that they would be visiting every day from now on. The team consisted of Liam, Trish, Mel, Sharni, Michelle and Melissa, who was a social worker.

She brought a red medicine box that would stay at the house, filled with various pain relief medications that Mario might need to start taking. The family was educated on how to administer morphine. Mario mentioned that, over the last couple of days, he had been getting headaches and his head hurt when he spoke. He didn't take anything for those headaches but knew the option of medication was there if he wanted it.

Later, Christine from the Red Cross came to give Mario a shower. As he sat and was washed by a stranger, water cascaded down his yellow skin, washing away another piece of his independence.

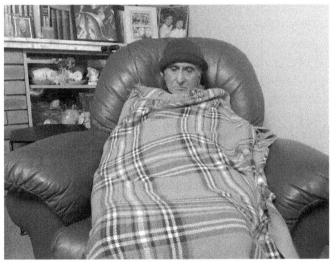

ABOVE: Mario sleeping on the couch,
too tired and weak to do anything.

10th August:

Mario couldn't be left alone anymore and Maria needed to go to the doctor's because she wasn't feeling any better in herself. Her bad cough was actually bronchitis and she had to return to the doctor's to get a further opinion on how to deal with it. With the condition she was in, the doctor suggested she be hospitalised so they could put her on a drip. Maria refused to go; how could she when her husband was dying at home? The timing couldn't have been worse and increased the already stressful situation.

A nurse came out in the morning but there wasn't much to do once he saw Mario was coping well. Liam was a tall English man, with a wonderful bedside manner and immediately established a good rapport with Mario.

'You're looking good, Mario,' Liam observed. 'I think you'll last longer than two weeks.'

The wish for more time was just that – a wish. But hearing that fanned the flame of hope again; maybe Mario would prove the doctor wrong.

While Maria was out, Suzanne, Gina and Catena stayed with Mario. They all sat in the lounge, watching the day pass them by. As Mario had company, he tried to stay awake but he couldn't fight the pull of his eyelids and he drifted in and out of sleep. When he woke up, he turned to see Suzanne still there, reading a magazine.

'Sorry, I can't stay awake.'

'That's okay, rest if you need to,' Suzanne reassured.

The situation must have been weighing on Mario, as he then said, 'I don't feel like I'm needed anymore. I just sit here and I'm drowsy all the time.'

'You're not giving up, are you?'

Mario shook his head and said, 'No, I'm not giving up. I'm still fighting.'

That afternoon, two workers from the hospital came to

the house to deliver Mario's hospital bed and a wheelchair. They had also brought a better walker, as Mario was finding his current walker difficult to manoeuvre. They set the bed up in the back room, ready for when Mario needed it. Having the equipment there made the reality of what was happening harder to ignore. Those symbols of loss of mobility and independence stood out glaringly. This was happening, whether the family liked it or not.

ABOVE: Mario enjoys some time with Emmy.

11th August:

Mario needed some pain relief – the ache in his stomach had come back. He had avoided strong painkillers up to this point, but it was now time to start using the powerful drugs. He had his first dose of morphine and found it alleviated his discomfort. The nurses had been very clear about Mario taking pain medication when he needed it. They told him their focus was to manage his pain and make him as comfortable as possible. Mario tended to not complain much and downplay his pain, but they encouraged him to be open and honest about how he was feeling. Mario agreed and promised to speak up if he was hurting.

The rest of the day passed by, Mario sleeping on the couch. The grandfather clock that had belonged to his mother ticked and tocked beside him. A steady rhythm, marking out the passage of time. That unstoppable cadence which accompanies us all yet for the vast majority of our lives we ignore, frittering away the precious seconds, that build to seemingly unending minutes, hours and days. Only when that rhythm is bringing us so close to the moment when the hands will stand still, do we realise how limited the ticks and the tocks are. Every hour, the clock would chime, yet another one passed by, never to be had again.

12th August:

In the space between the moon rising and falling, when darkness overwhelms the light, a lot can change. While some sleeping bodies dream and rejuvenate, others degenerate. Some wake refreshed, healthy and ready to start the day. Others struggle out of bed, bodies already weary. Mario woke that cold morning and felt the change within him. His physical strength was depleting quickly. His desire for food was gone. Once he would have woken with a healthy appetite, starting the day with a bowl of Weet-bix. He never skipped breakfast, or any meal for that matter. Today he did. Throughout the course of the day, barely any food passed his lips. The family knew how he loved his food, so to see him refusing to eat was difficult. Over the day, they'd ask him, 'Would you like anything to eat?'

When he'd reply, 'No thank you,' their hearts would sink. If they could get him to eat, maybe he would pick up. If he would eat, maybe they could still pretend that he was going to be fine.

Since it was clear Mario wouldn't make it to see Suzanne's children's book published, she had made a mock-up of it. Mario had been extremely proud when he found out Suzanne was getting a book published, as he knew that she had always been passionate about writing. But more so because the topic was close to their hearts. The book was about mental illness and Mario was pleased that Suzanne wanted to help other families who had been through what they had.

As Mario sat with two blankets pulled over him, Suzanne came and sat next to him.

'I've got something to show you,' she said.

Mario was feeling sleepy. He didn't say anything, but opened his eyes wider and smiled, showing his interest without having to exert too much energy.

'You know how you said you wanted to see my book come out, but we don't know if that will happen...'

Mario nodded and Suzanne continued.

'What I've done is, I've printed out a copy so you can at least see it.'

Suzanne picked up the book and brought it closer, holding up the colourful cover page for Mario to see.

'This is my children's book,' Suzanne revealed.

Mario looked at it, a faint smile touching his lips. In any normal circumstance, Mario would have showed a lot more enthusiasm. But it was hard when things were fading at the edges. It was hard to focus when his body needed to sleep.

He spoke softly. 'Thank you very much.'

She opened the book. 'This is the dedication. I've written: *"For Dad, and all the other families who have been touched by mental illness. You are not alone."'*

'What do you think?'

'Beautiful. Good effort, Suzanne.'

She could see he was tired. 'I'll read it to you another day.'

'Okay,' he replied.

He used all his strength to smile at her, offering her all he had at that time. She smiled in return, and then sat back in her chair. Not long after, Mario was asleep.

Mario did not get off the couch much that day, not even to go to the toilet. As night fell, the family realised that he had not been to the toilet in hours. Another sign that slowly, his body was shutting down.

ABOVE: Suzanne shows Mario a mock-up of her picture book, inspired by their journey with mental illness.

13th August:

Again, Mario missed breakfast. Liam came in the morning, noticing immediately the change in his patient. He could see that there had been further deterioration, the increased weakness and lethargy evident. The first dose of morphine worked effectively so at least Mario wasn't in pain, but the disease's progression was unmistakable. Maria informed Liam about the lack of appetite and the lack of a toilet visit in twenty-four hours. This concerned Liam and he warned that, if Mario still hadn't gone by mid-afternoon, he would need to come back and insert a catheter.

Before Liam left, he turned to Maria. 'I had thought that Mario would go longer than two weeks, but looking at him today, unfortunately I think the doctor was right with her prognosis.'

Liam had seen what the family had been witnessing over the last few days. Death had its grip on Mario; his spark that used to be so strong had flickered and was almost out. He still blessed everyone with his wide smile, but the light in his eyes had diminished. No longer animated, no longer talkative, he was a shell of his former self.

As Mario hadn't moved from the couch, and was finding it difficult to get up, it was clear the time had come to move him to the hospital bed. The workers had set up the bed in the back room but that would mean he would be secluded at the back of the house. This wasn't ideal, as Mario always loved to be part of everything that the family was doing. It was Gina who pointed this out and suggested they move the bed into the lounge room. The others had assumed it would be quieter if he was in the back room; able to rest more peacefully. But on thinking about it, it was obvious that this was a great idea. Mario would still be able to be a part of the family's comings and goings, and the lounge room could fit more people, so they all wouldn't have to cram in the small room at the back.

Luke and Jordan disassembled the bed, while the ladies rearranged furniture to make way for it. Reassembling it on Mario's favourite spot, where the couch had been, meant he could still see all the family photos that lined the walls, able to reminisce, to forget where he was and focus on where he had been. He could also look out the wide floor length window and watch the world continue on the outside, the one he used to be a part of, coming and going as he pleased.

Before Luke left to go back to Perth, he wheeled the walking frame over and said, 'Mario, I've put a bike bell on your walker. That way, if you need help in the middle of the night, you can reach out and ring it.'

Luke demonstrated and a sharp ping sounded.

Mario smiled. 'Ah, thank you, Luke. That's a good idea.'

Later Mario was able to eat a light lunch, but food was no longer a pleasurable experience; tastes and textures he had once enjoyed turned his stomach and made him scrunch up his nose in disgust. Luckily, he was eventually able to go to the toilet, the mere threat of a possible catheter seemingly getting his bowels and bladder to co-operate. For now, at least, Mario could avoid another reminder of his failing independence.

Helped into the hospital bed, he settled down into the mattress, carving his imprint into an unfamiliar spot and unknowingly bringing to an end so many of life's small, yet rich, experiences. No longer would he step foot outside his house or go to his beloved shed. No longer would he go and sit on the verandah, eating a piece of fruit and humming happily as he admired his garden. There would be no more afternoon naps on his familiar chair, no more nights spent in his own bed in his own room, with Maria sleeping beside him. He would never dress himself again, or sit at his desk and flip the calendar onto a new day. There would be no more breakfasts on the balcony, sitting alongside Maria at their table, listening to the birds sing their morning song. All those little things that were taken for granted were all of a sudden out of reach, experiences that were now only memories.

When news started to spread within the family that Mario didn't have long, a steady stream of visitors began to arrive. Family members came, wanting to see Mario and spend time with him. The phone rang more than ever. At times, the driveway looked like a car yard. Tears were shed every time someone new came through the door. Maria was still sick, unable to rest and get better, the stress no doubt making her recovery harder.

At one point, while Tony sat beside Mario's bed, keeping his brother company, Mario said softly, 'I don't want to be a burden on the family. I might as well go if I can't do much here.'

Most of the time, the words that came out of Mario's mouth were positive, hopeful. On the odd occasion when Mario's positivity would slip and doubt and uncertainty would take its place, it was almost a shock to hear. Completely out of character, but evidence that even someone with the strongest fighting spirit has their limits. Hope can take you far but, when death is staring you in the face, it is easy to lose grip, hopelessness threatening to overpower your positive mindset.

What Mario failed to see in that moment of frustration was that he was not a burden. Sure, it was hard and emotional, but the family hated seeing Mario so helpless. He wasn't a burden, because, even though it was tough, at least he was still here, in their presence. His presence was better than the alternative. Dealing with that would be a far harder load to carry.

ABOVE: Mario's first day in the hospital bed.

14th August:

Mario was able to sit up and have some breakfast, which pleased everyone. Surely if he was still able to eat, even if the portion was small, that meant that death had released its grip a little. Maybe eating would build up his strength, maybe he could fight the cancer that was eroding his insides.

He was also able to get up and use his walker to get to the bathroom. It was the first time he'd gone since the previous afternoon; the length of time between visits still not ideal. Anyone would burst at the very thought of holding on for that long, but it wasn't a matter of 'holding on' for Mario. Just the simple consequence of his organs not working how they should.

It was only a matter of time until Mario would no longer be able to manage the toilet by himself. He tried to keep this part of his independence for as long as he could. With weak arms, he had been able to slowly complete a task that he had been able to freely do for most of his life. But not today. Today the weakness pulling at his body was too much.

'Maria,' he called, loathing what he was about to ask his wife to do.

She appeared at the doorway, pausing for an instant, having also dreaded this eventuality. She wasn't a nurse and the thought of it made her squeamish.

After a moment though, she thought, *In sickness and in health*.

Mario hadn't chosen this; it was the last thing he wanted to ask of his wife. And Maria, having always stayed true to the vows she uttered a lifetime ago, helped Mario with what he could no longer do for himself.

Liam came mid-morning, and using an iPad set up a teleconference with Mario's palliative doctor.

'Hi Mario, how are you?' she asked with a friendly wave towards his beanie-clad head.

'Hi, Doctor,' Mario said quietly. 'I'm good, thanks.'

They spoke briefly but it was hard for Mario to hear. Before she was handed back to Liam, she asked, 'Mario, is there anything else I can do for you to make you more comfortable?'

'No, Doctor,' he answered. 'The nurses are doing a great job looking after me.'

'Great, I'm glad to hear that. Okay, well Mario, I'm not sure what else I can do for you at this end. I'll leave you in the nurses' care, but if you need anything, let me know. Goodbye, Mario. Good luck.'

'Thank you. Bye, Doctor.' Mario smiled at his friendly doctor one last time. They wouldn't speak again.

Before Liam ended the call, Suzanne signalled to Liam that she had a question.

'Based on the prognosis you gave when Dad last saw you, how do you think he is going? From what you've seen and heard, is there any chance he will go longer?'

Doctors must get used to their patients and their families asking questions that they can't answer. They get used to the desperation in the families eyes, pleading for them to give good news, a solid, definitive answer that would put an end to their questions. Realistically, Suzanne knew the answer wouldn't be definite, it could only be the doctor's assumption, based on experience and Mario's blood results. But, she must have heard the hope in Suzanne's question, mixed with the resignation of what couldn't be changed. Two conflicting emotions that fought against each other and which no doubt, palliative doctors must have seen each and every day.

So she answered with sympathy lacing her response, but also truthfully.

'He is doing better than I expected at this stage but I still think the same time frame.'

Liam ended the call, facing the dejected faces of Maria and Suzanne.

'I know it's hard to believe,' he began. 'I've seen people at the stage Mario is at and they are not eating at all or getting up to go to the toilet. Mario is doing pretty well considering. He is mostly symptom free at the moment, apart from his increasing weakness.'

'That's Mario,' Maria added, clearing the hard lump in her throat. 'He has never done anything by the book.'

Liam laughed. 'We'll call it the 'Mario Factor'.'

They all looked affectionately at Mario, who just flashed another of his smiles, nodding his approval at the label Liam had given him.

Mario seemed to pick up a little and was able to enjoy an afternoon filled with visitors. His brother, Robbie, and his wife, Angie came along with Tony and Wendy and their three girls. He sat up in his bed and was able to participate in the conversation. Tired but feeling at ease, Mario took advantage of his second-wind and got out of bed to sit upright in a chair. He posed for photos, looking straight into the camera lens and smiling widely. Were an outsider to look at that photo without knowing Mario's story, they would never guess that he had been in the last weeks of his life.

He was even able to sit at the dinner table that evening, and share a bowl of hot pumpkin soup with his family. It was the 'Mario Factor'; he had a way of beating the odds and fooling everyone into a false sense of security.

ABOVE: A precious family photo, back row – Matthew and Maria, front row – Suzanne, Mario and Stephanie.

ABOVE: Mario enjoying dinner at the table with his family.

ABOVE: Mario enjoying time with his family, from left – Laura, Nicole, Robbie, Mario, Angie, Wendy, Rebecca, Heath and Stephanie.

15th August:

Seeing a nurse everyday had become part of the family's routine, and already they had come to anticipate their visit, finding reassurance and understanding in their kind words and warm smiles. Things had seemed to plateau with Mario; there was nothing new to report.

Maria pulled Mel aside once she had seen to Mario.

'How will we know when it is time?' she asked quietly.

'There are usually signs. Sleeping more, hard to rouse. His breathing may change. Or it could be quick – you could wake up and find he slipped away in his sleep, or you could step outside for a bit and come back to find him gone. There's no way of saying for sure.'

It seemed to be the day for picking the nurse's brain. The family had wanted to have a special day spent with Mario, followed by a family dinner, since their plan to go away never eventuated. Abbey was there when the nurse visited, so she asked for Mel's opinion.

'We were planning a family get together and dinner, but my boys and myself were sick. We had to postpone and are thinking of having it this coming weekend. Do you think we could wait for the weekend, with the way things are going?'

Mel looked at Mario. 'If it was me I would be doing it sooner rather than later.'

Time was against them, so Matthew, Jordan and Stephanie arranged to have the next day off work, and a dinner menu was quickly organised. The family day was happening tomorrow, because Mario's tomorrows were quickly running out.

16th August:

Mario awoke, confused. The line between dreams and reality was blurred. When Maria and Stephanie went in to say good morning, he told them, 'Someone broke into the house. He put a pillow over my head and tried to smother me. Suzanne was here, too, and I saw Gina standing over me.'

Maria and Stephanie looked at each other, taken aback. The way Mario spoke, it sounded like he actually thought this had happened.

'Don't worry, Dad,' Stephanie reassured. 'It was just a dream, no one broke in.'

Mario looked up at the ceiling. 'Oh, okay,' he mumbled, closing his eyes.

Not long after, Suzanne came over, pulling a suitcase behind her. She waited for Mario to wake up, and then greeted him. Mario smiled at his daughter as she leant over to hug him. It was awkward hugging whilst lying down so he couldn't return the hug properly. It wasn't too long ago that Mario would wait at the door, watching Suzanne walk up the steps. As soon as she opened the door, he would be there, arms wide, smiling, reaching out to hug her hello.

'How are you feeling, Dad?'

'Not bad,' he replied softly. 'I'm feeling better today. I think I've got over the worst of it.'

'That's good,' Suzanne said, hiding her sadness. Was that his usual positive self? Did he actually believe he would recover, or was he in denial? No one wanted to crush his spirit, so the few times he said statements like that, no one dared to correct him. Who were they to take away the last bit of hope he had left? False hope was better than no hope.

'Guess what? I'm sleeping over tonight. I'm going to stay here with you guys for a while.'

Mario smiled. 'Lovely,' he said. 'How long for?'

'As long as you need, Dad. I want to be here with you.'

'Lovely,' he said again, appreciation evident in his eyes.

In the early afternoon, Jordan and Emmy came over, as well as Matthew, Abbey, Jesaia and Coby. While the kids played outside, the family sat around Mario's bedside, playing music to him. Matthew played an old Italian song, *C'e La*

Luna Mezz'o Mare. Mario would always go around the house singing that one phrase, over and over, because he couldn't remember the words to the rest of the song. He listened intently, a smile playing on his lips the whole time.

'We need wine,' Mario joked, his words mumbled and low.

Everyone laughed, glad to see he still had his humour. The song finished and Mario started struggling to keep his eyes open. They let him sleep for a while, and then Maria woke him. Matthew and Suzanne had compiled some videos of Mario with his grandchildren over the years, and they planned to play them on the TV for him to relive those special moments. Maria gently shook his arm.

'Mario,' she called. 'Wake up. We want to show you some videos.'

He was hard to wake and it took a few attempts to rouse him. It was supposed to be a special time, watching the videos together. Instead, Mario didn't take much of it in, struggling to stay awake. The others watched, tears clouding their vision. They wished they could have that Mario back again. If only they could see him hugging and talking and interacting with his grandchildren like he used to. Mario was trying to focus but the images kept blurring as his eyes rolled around. Eventually, he fell asleep, and the family didn't have the heart to wake him when he so clearly needed sleep more than he needed a trip down memory lane.

Later that afternoon, he did waken and for the first time that day, got up. He moved slowly, his muscles weak from being bedridden. He made his way to the dining table and sat down in his usual spot. Maria made him a cup of tea and he sipped at it slowly, using a straw because that was easier now. Suzanne sat beside him, savouring the moment of sharing a cup of tea with her Dad, at the table, just like they used to. Stephanie was sitting alone in the lounge room and Mario had a clear view of her from where he was sitting. He looked at her and then asked Suzanne, 'Who is that sitting next to Stephanie?'

The nurses had said that Mario might get confused as the toxins continued to build up and his body couldn't break them down. If this happened years ago, the family would have been concerned that Mario was having a relapse of his mental illness. If just a hallucination, then it was clear that he was one step closer to the end.

'No one's there, Dad. It's just Steph,' she reassured, putting her hand on his arm.

As dinnertime approached, Gina and Catena arrived. Mario was still sitting at the table, the longest he'd been out of bed in a while. Food was placed on the table, a feast that he once would have devoured wholeheartedly. Lasagne, cutlets, garlic bread, salad, eggplant and chicken wings were on offer, the house filled with the aroma of good food. He hadn't eaten much that day and wasn't particularly hungry, but he made himself finish the small piece of lasagne and serving of salad that was on his plate. The mood was happy, conversation flowed freely and noise filled the room. It was just like the meals the family used to share and they could all pretend for that meal, at least, that things weren't about to change dramatically.

After the meal was over, Mario stayed at the table for as long as he could, enjoying everyone's company. But the willpower and strength he needed to finish the meal at the table had gone.

'Thank you for the meal everyone. I enjoyed it. Can I go back to bed now, please?'

Matthew helped him up and led him over to the bed. When Matthew had assisted him into the bed and put the blankets over him, tucking him in for the night, Mario let out a relieved sigh.

'Ah, I made it!' he exclaimed, proud that he was able to summon up enough strength to get through the meal. He knew it was important for his family to have that time with him and he was glad he was able to give them that.

That meal was the last the family ever shared with Mario. The significance of it not realised at the time, but cherished in the days to come. He would never sit at that table again, nor say, 'Bon Appétit!' at the start of every dinnertime. From that point on, Mario would be fully confined to his bed, only getting up to go to the toilet.

LEFT: Mario and Suzanne enjoy a cup of tea together.

RIGHT: Mario's last meal shared at the dinner table with his family.

17th August:

After the effort it took Mario to participate in the previous night's meal, he spent most of the day sleeping. He had a small breakfast, but no lunch or dinner. When his mouth was dry, he would have sips of water, as well as some juice and a few mandarins. His body was no doubt under strain from the meal he had eaten the previous evening, working hard to digest the food.

It was a quiet day, broken up by a visit from Armando and Connie, who had travelled from Perth. They had been a wonderful support when Mario had had his brain bleed. More recently, Armando had been a great brother, driving down from Perth every few weeks to take Mario out for a coffee. Mario loved those times and when he saw them come through the door, he was very pleased. Armando tried to disguise the sadness he felt when he saw his brother lying there; it seemed there had been so much change in such a short time. They chatted together, Mario mostly listening because the tiredness was making it difficult to focus. When they could see Mario was struggling to stay awake, they kissed him goodbye and left, hoping they could make it down to see him again.

That afternoon, when Matthew finished work, he brought over an electric shaver. Mario's hair, the little he had left, had been growing and although always hidden by a beanie, he liked to keep it short.

Matthew sat him up in bed, placed a towel over him and put his hairdressing skills to the test. He shaved the hair short, which made Mario's head look smaller. The soft, bald patch at the top of his head, once skin colour, was now yellow. It seemed somehow fitting that, for his last haircut, his son was the one who was able to do it for him.

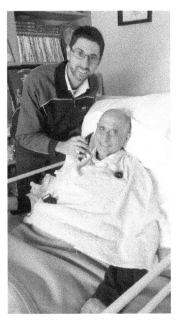

ABOVE: Matthew gives Mario his last haircut.

With people coming and going, it was hard for Mario and Maria to get time alone. That evening, Suzanne and Stephanie left them, and Maria brought a chair over and sat beside Mario. These days, it was difficult to have a lengthy conversation with Mario. But meaningful discussions couldn't wait so Maria took a deep breath and tried to convey her deepest feelings packed into a few sentences.

'I'm sorry if sometimes I wasn't a good wife.'

Mario quietly responded, 'It's okay, Darling. You have been a good wife. Thank you for looking after me. No one could have done it better.'

Maria fought back tears as she finally found the courage to give Mario permission to let go if he wanted to.

'The kids' and I will be okay if you have had enough of fighting and want to go be with Jesus.'

'I'll pick up and get through this,' he offered. He was powerless to stop this disease, but he was still not ready to leave his family. His mind was fighting against his body, wrestling an invisible and unbeatable force. Mario's love was the fuel that powered his fight and he was giving it all he had.

Maria sadly replied, 'We would love you to get better but unfortunately that won't happen.'

With the sad truth settled between them, Mario's eyes drifted shut, unable to stay awake any longer.

18th August:

Mario's food intake had decreased dramatically; on this day totalling only two mandarins and a piece of quiche. He had always liked the sweet fruit and it seemed that as his appetite diminished, his enjoyment of fruit hadn't. When he would turn up his nose at the offer of most foods, he'd nod his head at the suggestion of a mandarin.

He was still drinking water, but not as much as before.

Trish came to check on him and found there wasn't much she could do. So far he had been an easy patient and hadn't required anything more than the routine visits they provided each day. Just before she was about to leave, she looked at Mario. He returned her gaze and smiled. She couldn't help but smile back and said, affectionately, 'Oh, Mario, you beautiful man!'

Maria was standing by Mario's bed, enjoying the exchange between nurse and patient. Trish turned to Maria, and with complete genuineness said, 'Mario is such a wonderful man. You know, each time we visit him we'll go back to the office and say how wonderful he is. It's his beautiful smile; the way he looks you in the eye and his whole face lights up.'

As Maria listened to the heart-warming compliments, tears glistened in her eyes. She looked down at Mario and in a shaky voice, replied, 'Yes, he is a special man. He will leave a hole, that's for sure.'

The emotion spilled over, Trish's kind words about this humble man striking a cord. Reminding Maria that those lovable qualities which made Mario unique were soon to be lost.

That afternoon the rain relentlessly bucketed down, like an ominous premonition of the tears that would be spilt. Mario's nephews, Claudio and Sandro, came to visit. Mario was excited to see them and managed to stay awake to reminisce with them about their younger days. Sandro took Mario back to the days when his knowledge and expertise were sought, and chatted about the many hours spent fixing motorbikes. They talked about cars and tools until Mario's eyes began to droop, signalling it was time to let him rest. They hugged and said goodbye and when they were at the door ready to leave, Mario called out, 'When I'm better I'd like to visit you again.'

Sandro and Claudio looked at their uncle and said, 'That'll be nice, Uncle Mario.' As they bent their heads ready to battle the rain outside, Mario watched them leave, his hope trailing behind them.

19th August:

Mario was surrounded by family all day; being a Saturday, the work week over, meant the men could also spend some time with Mario. Luke, who was down from Perth, Matthew and his family, along with Suzanne and her family, filled the spaces of Mario's home with happy noise. Even from his bed, Mario rejoiced in his family being under the one roof. Their energy changed the atmosphere of the place. If it wasn't for the hospital bed that Mario was laying in, a visual reminder of his fate, it could have just been a normal lazy

Saturday, no eyes on the clock. Mario gathered enough strength to stay awake for a couple of hours and managed, throughout the day, to eat breakfast, a nagatale – an Italian biscuit shaped like a plait, a cup of tea, a glass of coke, and sips of water.

By mid-afternoon, Mario ran out of steam. As the rest of the family did their own thing, he couldn't stay awake and fell asleep to the soundtrack of their voices, floating around him and working their way into his dreams, so he still felt a part of the family.

20th August:

It had been one week since Mario became bed-bound. One week since he had stepped outside, breathed fresh air, and had freedom to walk to the fridge when he was hungry. He had stared at the same four walls for seven days straight. He had carved his imprint into his deathbed, whilst in what had been his normal bed, next to Maria, the memory of his shape lingered.

He hadn't complained once, even though he could only lie on his back and needed help to roll onto his side. This position wasn't ideal, because it put a lot of pressure on his enlarged spleen and liver, so he mostly lay on his back, staring at the ceiling.

His family had offered at various times to help him into the wheelchair so they could take him to sit on the verandah. Mario always declined, no longer interested in the outside world.

Trish visited again, bringing with her more compliments for Mario. He looked up at her, smiling. She held his gaze, returning the smile.

'Mario,' she gushed. 'You have eyes a woman can drown in.'

Maria, Suzanne and Stephanie were in the lounge room when she said this, and they all laughed affectionately. Mario cast his head down and lowered his eyes, as if bashful about the attention. Then he looked up and smiled, his bright eyes framed by his long eyelashes.

Trish, with her wonderful bedside manner, had a way of reminding Mario that even though he was bedridden, he still had the power to have an impact on those around him.

Later that day, Mario needed to visit the bathroom. Maria and Suzanne stood on either side of him and helped him sit. He took some deep breaths, and looked at the walker in front of him. He gripped the handles and slowly pushed himself up, steadying himself, a look of concentration on his face.

'I feel like I've forgotten how to walk,' he admitted.

'Just take it slow, Dad. One step at a time,' Suzanne encouraged.

He took another deep breath and pushed forward, taking Suzanne's advice. He moved at a snail's pace, his tongue poking from his mouth, the way he always did when he was focused on something. For Mario, walking was no longer a natural unconscious act. Now, it was a battle; a conscious effort to remind the brain that his feet needed to move. *One step at a time*, he thought, as he stared at his feet and focused on the path ahead.

Apart from the breakfast Mario ate that morning, he only had three mandarins and a few glasses of water. When night closed in, his stomach wasn't growling in hunger. Instead, something else growled deep in his belly; a vicious monster that had been eating away at him and was just waiting for the moment to deliver its final, fatal bite.

21st August:

It was a quiet start to a new week, and after the full house over the weekend, it seemed a bit empty. Mario spent most of the day sleeping, waking intermittently, each time finding the hands of the clock in a different position. One time he woke to find Emmy dressed up as Snow White. The vision made him smile; her young, joyful exuberance as she played make-believe a welcome distraction to his story. As she played, Maria and Suzanne helped him sit up.

He smiled at his granddaughter. 'You look beautiful, Emmy.'

She paraded over to him. 'I'm Snow White, Nonno,' she said proudly.

Suzanne quickly reached for her phone, wanting to capture the moment. Mario put his hand on Emmy's shoulder and they both smiled at the camera. Mario, in his flannelette pajamas and red beanie, and Emmy in her dress and crown. The last photo they ever had taken together.

By the end of the day, Mario had only eaten three pieces of licorice, three pikelets and a handful of chips at dinner. As each day passed, his food intake decreased. Mario's flesh, hidden by his clothes, had become looser, his skinny shoulder blades poking out.

LEFT: *The last photo Mario and Emmy had together.*

22nd August:

Mario woke, a grimace on his face. Maria heard him stirring and went to him.

'Morning, Mario. How are you?'

He turned his head slowly, unable to greet her with a smile like he usually did.

'Darling, my feet, back and stomach are hurting.'

Suzanne was close by so she and Maria tried to re-position Mario, adjusting the hospital bed in an effort to ease his discomfort.

Luckily, a nurse came round shortly after and was able to administer two milligrams of morphine. It didn't take long for the drug to ease his pain. His face relaxed and he was able to go back to sleep.

Matthew dropped by on his lunch break. Mario was pleased to see his son and managed to stay awake the whole time that Matthew was there. Maria, Suzanne and Stephanie also sat around his bed, Mario savouring this time with his family. They chatted about Mario's memories, his deceased mother, who was always in Mario's thoughts. They showed him photos of the past and reminisced.

Suzanne was leaning over the bed, having just showed him a photo, when he said, 'I'll pick up...how long have I been in bed?'

'Just over a week, Dad,' Suzanne answered.

Staring up at the ceiling, he said, as if to himself, 'Life changes so quickly.'

Suzanne nodded. 'Do you know why you're in bed?'

'No,' he said, shaking his head.

'It's because you have liver cancer, Dad.'

Mario's eyes widened, a look of shock crossing his face. His mouth opened, giving a silent answer. Mario's mind was becoming foggier, his thoughts clouded. The sense of reality and time evading him. He was trying hard to hold on, but it was getting more and more difficult.

Matthew's lunch break was up; regretfully he had to go back to work.

Everyone could see Mario fading, so each goodbye was treated like it could be the last. Like a magic trick, he could be here one minute, gone the next. They became emotion filled, not rushed like most goodbyes are. Words from the heart were not left unsaid, because no one could guarantee if they would get a next time to say them.

Matthew leant down, his hand on Mario's arm. He looked him in the eye as he said, 'Goodbye. I'm so proud of you, Dad. I'm thankful you are my Dad. You'll always hold a special place in my heart. I love you very much.'

Mario smiled up at Matthew. 'Goodbye, son.'

After Matthew had left, and Mario was sleeping, Maria admitted to Suzanne and Stephanie what she had been feeling. She was aware that Mario had eaten and drank even less this day, having only had two mandarins.

'I could be wrong, but I've had a feeling today that he doesn't have long left.'

They had all known his prognosis, and it had already been two weeks since the doctor gave him the timeframe of a week or two. It was unsettling that it could now only be a matter of days, or hours. It didn't bear thinking about.

In the late afternoon, while Tony, Gina and Catena were over, the community home-care nurse came to give Mario a shower. They had been coming every few days, and Mario looked forward to it. As tiring as it was to get out of bed, he always felt refreshed after a warm shower and fresh clothes. Mario had begun to smell, even though he didn't sweat and wasn't doing anything to get dirty. Even after his shower, though, his skin still gave off a foul odour. Maria had asked the nurses about this, and they explained that it wasn't because Mario was dirty. It was due to the amount of toxins that were now in his body. His liver was unable to break down the proteins and this illustrated that he was in the advanced stages of liver disease.

When Maria helped undress Mario, it shocked and saddened her to see his skeletal frame, except for his large, protruding belly. His skin, now yellow from head to toe. Cancer transforms the body, making loved ones look almost unrecognisable. The damage was hidden under Mario's clothes, but when he was stripped bare, the ugly truth of his disease hit home.

ABOVE: No matter what, Mario still manages to smile.

23rd August:

Mario managed to get up and go to the bathroom. He was able to sit up in bed for a short time and ate two mandarins, two nagatales and a glass of apple juice. He hadn't complained of any more pain since the previous day. Every morning that the sun rose and Mario's eyes opened was a blessing. He had lived past the prognosis predicted by his doctor. He had kept everyone guessing, the ball of dread sitting in his family's bellies, growing bigger as each day passed. He had the 'Mario Factor'. He was weak, but everyone who saw the fight he was putting up, could only describe him as strong.

24th August:

The weakness that Mario felt had intensified further. It had become harder for him to move, to eat, to talk. Trying to do so made him even weaker; it was like a heavy force was pushing down on him, keeping him prisoner in the bed.

His heels were aching. It was no wonder, seeing as they had been rubbing and resting in the same spot for over a week. When the nurse came, she stuck some pads in place to take some pressure off.

Amazingly, later that day, when the community home-care nurse came, he found the willpower to get up, even though his body felt heavy and sluggish. The nurse could see the change and she worked patiently and gently with him, allowing him to take as much time as he needed. The warm water, normally soothing, felt like sharp jabs. He gritted his teeth as the rush of water ran over his tender skin. When the water stopped he was immediately cold. It was a relief when he flopped back into bed and had the covers pulled over him, cocooning him once again.

'Ah,' he let out a whoosh of air, struggling to get his breath back after the exertion.

He still thanked the lady who had kindly washed him, never forgetting his manners even in his state. When she had left, he said to Maria, 'Darling, I feel even weaker when I move my head or talk.'

'Just rest now,' Maria soothed.

He stared at the ceiling; the pattern of the roof etched into his brain by now, then closed his eyes, hoping that when he woke again, he would have gathered some strength.

By the end of the day, Mario had only eaten a mandarin and a nagatale. He had only drank a glass of milk and another of apple juice. Water no longer had the same appeal. It now tasted strange to Mario and he began to wonder how he had ever enjoyed eating and drinking. His life pre-hospital bed seemed like a distant dream; his abilities and independent life now out of reach. In his mind, he tried calling to the old Mario but it was too late, he was gone. All that lay ahead was his new reality, a journey he had to face with bravery and faith.

25th August:

It had been a long night for Mario. While everyone slept, he lay in the dark, suffering in silence. He couldn't see the time, which made the minutes drag even slower. When light started to stream through the gaps in the curtains he knew the sun had risen. Shadows started to retreat, the light chasing away the dark. He lay for a while longer, not having the energy to call out or move. The discomfort was intense. He heard noise; signs that the household was now awake. Mario tried to speak the words that perched on his lips, but all that came out was a mumble. A groan. Footsteps approached. He turned his head to find Suzanne standing there.

'Are you okay, Dad?' she asked, leaning close.

Clearing his throat, he tried to speak again. Softly, slowly, the words came.

Scrunching up his face, he said, 'I'm in terrible pain. I've been uncomfortable for hours and I'm freezing. My stomach and shoulders hurt.' Mario exhaled; the effort to speak took his breath away.

'Oh, Dad,' Suzanne said. 'You should have rung the bell and we would have come to help you.'

'I forget to ring the bell sometimes,' he whispered.

'It's okay, Dad. I'll give you some morphine, hopefully that will help.'

He closed his eyes, trying to shut out the pain. The next minute, Suzanne was gently pulling his sleeve up and emptying a vial of morphine into the port that was inserted into his arm.

'There you go, Dad. Just relax. You should feel better soon.'

'Thank you,' he mumbled. The corners of his mouth twitched. He wanted to smile, but his natural reaction became foreign in that moment. So he closed his eyes and waited for the morphine to mask the pain.

Later that morning, he awoke, dazed and drowsy. A tickle irritated his throat; his mouth parched. He coughed, his muscles contracting and building pressure inside his chest. The action immediately clouded his vision and made his head spin.

Groaning, he called desperately, 'Maria! Suzanne!'

Never far away, they ran to him.

'What's wrong, Mario?' Maria asked, her heart hammering.

'It hurts to cough,' he groaned.

Mario stared up at them, helplessness reflected in his eyes. All Maria and Suzanne could do was try to soothe him with their words. They were just as helpless, unable to take away his suffering and stress. All they could do was be there, to let him know he wouldn't have to face this difficult journey alone.

'Do you want a drink, Dad?'

'No thanks.'

'Then I can wet your lips with a cotton bud. Do you want me to do that?'

'Yes please.'

Suzanne went over to the medical box and found the mouthwash and a cotton tip. Once wet, she gently put the cotton tip to Mario's lips. He opened his mouth slightly and obediently, like a baby bird willingly waiting to be fed and looked after. The liquid made his lips shiny, a temporary balm. His tongue circled around, trying to draw the moisture into his mouth.

'There you go,' Suzanne said.

Sleepiness was dragging him down again, so Maria and Suzanne left him to rest as best as he could.

In the early afternoon, Mario felt the urge to use his bowels. Feeling extremely weak, he wondered how he would make it to the bathroom. Maria and Suzanne helped him up. Each step was a process. Following every movement there was a pause. Getting to the bathroom was like a marathon; dizziness and breathlessness made it a gruelling effort. Once in the bathroom, Suzanne gave them privacy, and let them do what needed to be done. Maria noticed, under the bright light, that Mario had become even more yellow.

When he was finished, and Maria had helped him, he washed his hands. Maria stood right beside him, her hand behind his back, ready to catch him if he fell. He wiped his hands, and while doing so, he uttered four words. Not to Maria, even though she was the only other person there with him.

Softly spoken, but clear as anything, he declared, 'I love you, God.'

Shivers rippled down Maria's spine. Mario, finding strength from above, made his way back to his bed. Once settled under the sheets, he tried to catch his breath.

'Ah…my chest…hurts.'

'Good effort, Dad,' Suzanne encouraged. 'You did really well.'

Maria and Suzanne left the room to let him rest again. They looked at each other. Both had seen the massive effort that it took for Mario to get up to use the bathroom.

'Might be time for a catheter,' Suzanne mused.

'Maybe,' Maria agreed. 'He won't like that.'

A few days earlier, when Mario had been talking with Tony, they were reminiscing about the foods their mother used to make. Mario had mentioned that he loved it when his mum would make roasted pears. Maria had overheard the conversation and decided that today would be the day to re-create her mother-in-law's delicious treat.

She went to Mario and offered him a piece of his past. The smell wafted to his nostrils. A smile softened his face, an image playing in his mind: his mother baking in the kitchen as he skirted around her, with the eagerness of a young boy with a rumbling belly.

'Thank you, Darling.'

He managed to eat half a roasted pear, washed down with a glass of apple juice. The memory he formed from eating the sweet treat was more enjoyable than the fruit itself. His appetite had changed dramatically to when he was a boy, asking for seconds and thirds.

It seemed fitting that, as that was the last thing he ate, he thought of his late mother. The one who had given him life, and to whom he would be reunited with soon.

After a brief rest, Mario woke, agitated once again. He complained of shoulder pain, so Suzanne gave him another dose of morphine. The mid-day sun streamed through the window, reminding them all that there was still light outside.

An hour and a half later, Mario's chest was hurting. More morphine was given. It was the last vial in the medical box, so Maria called the nurse to get some more. They had to come to the house to draw it up as per their procedures.

The community home-care nurse came, ready to shower Mario. He looked at her and shook his head.

'Sorry, I don't feel like having a shower.'

She could see the tension on the family's faces, she noticed that Mario looked worse than the last time she had come. She couldn't shower Mario, so she set up helping in other ways: wiping the dishes, tidying up, chatting to the family to distract them from the worry they felt. Once her time was up, she said goodbye to the family, sensing she wouldn't be needed there again.

Liam and Trish then arrived and went to assess Mario. They drew up more morphine and chatted to Maria about the situation. It was clear things were starting to intensify.

Since Mario missed his shower, they thought it would be nice to give him a bed bath. The family dispersed, giving them privacy. Ever so gently, Liam and Trish worked together to move Mario and take off his pajamas. He moaned and groaned, their gentle hands feeling rough on his tender skin. They dabbed the warm cloth over his emaciated, yellow limbs and over his swollen stomach. It was meant to be a refreshing experience, but to Mario, the movement was making him extremely uncomfortable. They re-dressed the top half of him, leaving the bottom half bare.

'Mario,' Liam called gently. 'I think it's time we put a catheter in.'

Mario's eyes widened. He shook his head. 'No,' was all he could manage.

'I know you don't want to, Mario, but we can see it is getting too difficult for you to get out of bed. This way, you won't have to worry about getting up.'

Never one to be a difficult patient, and not having the energy to protest any further, Mario nodded, showing his approval.

Before long, Mario had a catheter in place, as well as an adult diaper, pulled over the tube to protect it from rubbing on the blanket. The independent, capable Mario would have been embarrassed by the fact that he was wearing a nappy. But as it was, he was at a point where he didn't even have the energy to dwell on the fact. His pride and dignity about his physical capabilities was no longer an issue; he was quickly losing control, powerless to stop the fury of his disease.

That night, Mario didn't have to sleep alone. Maria, sensing that Mario was close to the end, brought her pillow and blanket and slept on the couch.

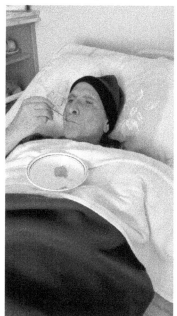

LEFT: *Mario eats his last 'meal'*
– roasted pear.

26th August:

Mario had held on through the night and made it to see another Saturday. Confused thoughts ran through his head. Maria and Suzanne sat beside him, nervous to leave now he was displaying signs that he was nearing the end.

Getting dreams mixed up with reality, he said, 'Mum made cake, then God made cake.' Or maybe, Mario knew that they were waiting for his imminent arrival.

Mario longed to talk the way he used to, but it was difficult to formulate sentences and string them together. He hated that Maria and Suzanne were sitting there looking at him, and he had nothing to offer them.

He managed to say, 'Thank you. I love you all.'

'We love you, too,' Suzanne answered.

Moments passed. Mario stared at the ceiling, transfixed, as if there was something up there that no one else could see.

'What are you thinking about?' Maria asked.

'I'm thinking about my recovery...I've been here for three weeks now.'

'It's only been two weeks, but no doubt it feels longer,' Maria corrected.

Mario fidgeted, his hands moving to his groin. He needed to scratch at the catheter.

'This catheter is uncomfortable. I need to do wees but I might get wet.'

'No, Dad, you won't get wet. It goes inside the tube...I bet it is annoying,' Suzanne added, sympathetically.

Mario was still agitated by the catheter when Trish came for her visit. She re-adjusted the tube, hoping that might help.

'Our aim now is purely to keep him comfortable,' Trish explained. 'If the catheter is still bothering him, give him some morphine.'

'Trish, from what you see, how long do you think Dad has left?' Suzanne asked, her voice low.

Trish paused, and looked at Mario. 'I can't say for sure, especially as your dad has the 'Mario Factor', but I wouldn't be surprised if I got a call from you guys tonight. I'm sorry, but you're possibly only looking at days now.'

Days. A day goes by in a flash. To be down to a matter of days, possibly hours, was unbelievable.

'I'm sorry,' Trish repeated, making her way to the door. 'Call me if you need me, for anything.'

It turned out that they did have to call Trish back. Mario had been suffering all morning; even a dose of morphine did not work. His agitation was increasing and it was getting unbearable for him to cope. Trish came back with some numbing cream. But after seeing how much discomfort the catheter was causing, and knowing Mario hadn't really wanted it in the first place, Maria asked if it was possible to remove it.

'That's no problem, I'll remove it. But Mario will still have to wear an adult diaper.'

'That will be better than a catheter,' Maria said, knowing Mario would prefer that option.

When Trish pulled out the long tube, Mario cried out in pain. Distressed and in agony, Mario writhed on the bed.

'Sorry, Mario,' Trish apologised. 'Now that it's out, you should feel much more comfortable.'

She was right; after some initial tenderness and irritation to the area, the pain subsided and Mario, utterly exhausted, fell asleep.

In the afternoon, Matthew, Abbey, Jesaia and Coby came to spend the afternoon. Matthew held a cake in his hands. It was Abbey's birthday. A day where normally the family would celebrate, light up candles and sing to commemorate another year of life. But today, the house was filled with heavy hearts and no one was in the mood to celebrate. Matthew cut a piece of cake for everyone and they ate it as they sat around Mario's bed. He slept on, as the family tried to swallow the cake despite the lump in their throats.

Around mid-afternoon, Armando arrived, having driven down from Perth.

'How is he today?' he asked, as Maria hugged him.

'He's not doing too well, Armando. I don't think he has long now.' Her voice cracked at the end.

Armando went to Mario, his eyes glistening with tears when he saw him.

'Hi, Mario.'

He sat alongside his silent brother, waiting for him to wake up and give him one of his trademark smiles.

'Sorry, Armando,' Maria apologised. 'You've driven all this way and he is sleeping. He's been this way all afternoon.'

'That's okay. At least I've been able to see him.'

While Armando conversed with the family, Mario's eyes fluttered open. He turned his head, a familiar voice filling his ears.

'Armando,' he whispered, a faint smile turning the corners of his mouth.

'Hi, Mario,' Armando said, standing up to get closer. 'Nice to see you.'

Mario nodded. It was nice to see Armando's face and he wanted to talk, but the tiredness was pulling him down.

'Thanks for coming,' Mario murmured.

They talked for a short time, the conversation mostly one-sided. Then Mario fell back to sleep, and Armando sat back down, watching Mario closely. Some time passed and it was clear that he wouldn't be able to converse with his brother again.

'I better go, Maria,' he said. 'I need to get home before it gets dark.'

'Of course,' Maria answered.

Armando leaned down and pressed his lips to Mario's forehead. 'Goodbye, Mario.'

Mario felt the warmth of Armando's lips on his head. He forced his eyes to open.

'I have to go now, Mario. You know, I will always remember our days working together…I love you.'

Mario smiled at Armando, his eyes flashing in recognition. Reminded of the days they worked side by side at the Power Station, their brotherly bond fueled by their shared love of machinery and fixing things. Those memories floated around in his mind but then became distant as sleep threatened to take over. Before he succumbed, he managed to whisper back to Armando.

'I love you too.' He stared at Armando's face until it became blurry, then he closed his eyes.

Armando stood straight, his hand on Mario's arm; one final connection. Armando gave one last look and then turned, his hand cupping his mouth as tears fell onto his cheeks. Maria walked him to the door, and hugged him. She was crying too as they said goodbye to each other. They both knew that the next time they would see each other would be at Mario's funeral.

Tony arrived around late afternoon, his usual time for visiting Mario. He was still sleeping, so Tony's visit was much like Armando's. Mario's ability to hold a conversation had gone, much like his ability to stay awake. Tony sat by his bed and quickly realised that he wouldn't be answering a multitude of questions from his interested brother again. He wouldn't be able to talk to him about the work he'd been doing, or discuss manly things like trailers and tools and cars.

'Mario asked about you yesterday, Tony,' Maria said. 'He wanted to know where you were.'

Tony gave a sad smile. 'It's a shame we didn't get to talk

much today. I came ready to answer more questions.'

'It's strange to see him so quiet,' Maria said.

Tony nodded, sighed and stood up. 'I guess I better go and let you have your dinner.'

He turned to face Mario, who was still sleeping. Like Armando, he leant down and hugged him. Mario stirred, and hoping he would hear, Tony said his final goodbye.

'Mario, I love you. Thanks for being a good brother.' He took a breath, cheeks wet and heart racing. Through his sobs, he managed one last word. 'Goodbye.'

He left quickly, before the full extent of his emotion overwhelmed him.

Conversation was scarce at the dinner table. The family ate their meal quickly. It felt wrong, eating a warm meal when Mario hadn't eaten all day. All he had managed was a glass of apple juice. They needed to nourish their bodies, but it still felt unfair when Mario was lying in the next room, dying. Stephanie and Luke finished first, so they went to the lounge room to be with Mario. They sat in the dark, the kitchen light providing enough illumination for them to see. Both were sitting quietly, when Mario suddenly opened his eyes.

'I love you, God,' Mario said. His eyes closed just as quick, as if that moment never happened. Stephanie and Luke stared at him, then stared at each other. Not long after, Mario said those same four words again. His eyes remained closed as he spoke.

After dinner, the family gathered around the bedside. The air had grown heavy and the mood was somber. Everyone felt the heaviness closing in. They watched Mario's every movement, every turn of the head. They felt his death was near so they waited, their chests tight as they felt the enormity of what was happening to their beloved Mario. He was restless and kept waking up. He saw his family standing around him, smiling at him each time he looked their way.

The adults talked softly every now and then with strained voices. The children's bubbly voices mixed with their tense tones and diluted the pressure in the air. Amongst their chatter, the clock ticked above them, rhythmic and never-ending.

Each time Mario would wake up, he would summon the energy to talk. Only a few words at a time, as if he needed to rest before he spoke again. When he would start murmuring, indicating he was speaking, everyone would lean forward, intent to hear what he had to say.

'Things will be back to normal tomorrow.'

'Thank you.'

'I have faith in you, God.'

'I'm glad I'm not in pain anymore.'

But he was restless and continuously moved in an effort to get comfortable.

Maria was at the head of the bed, as close to Mario as she could get. Her hand rested on his head while her thumb gently stroked his forehead. Back and forth, up and down. Trying to soothe his agitation. He turned to Stephanie, who was on the other side of him.

'It's hard to say this...'

Everyone leaned in. They held their breath, expecting an epiphany, some meaningful last words. He continued. 'I'm feeling very annoyed.' He paused, then turned to Maria.

'Darling, can you get your hand off my head please?'

Everyone let out the air they had been holding. They all broke into a fit of laughter. For a moment, it cut through the highly charged situation and lightened the mood. Mario managed a big smile. The old Mario had shone through, his funny way of putting things never failed to make his family laugh, even in the most dire of situations.

After about an hour of everyone standing around in the dark, Matthew and Abbey had to leave to get Jesaia and Coby to bed. Jordan and Emmy were staying over, and he had to put Emmy to bed too.

Matthew spoke. 'Dad, we've got to go now. The kids want to say goodnight.'

The three grandchildren stood in a line; their beautiful faces all staring at their Nonno.

They each said goodnight, their soft voices like music to Mario's ears.

Mario smiled and replied softly, 'Goodnight. I love you…God loves you too.'

It was hard for Matthew and Abbey to leave, not knowing how the night would unfold. They hugged Mario and told him they loved him.

'See you tomorrow, okay, Dad?'

Mario nodded. Matthew turned to Maria.

'Please call me straightaway if there's any change. I'll come back straight away.'

'I will, Matthew,' Maria answered. 'Hopefully I won't have to.'

Later on, when it was time to go to bed, Suzanne went to say goodnight to Mario. She gently nudged his arm and his eyes fluttered open. She gave him her best smile.

'I'm going to bed, Dad. See you in the morning, yeah?'

Mario looked at Suzanne. 'You're great.'

'So are you, Dad. I love you.'

She, along with everyone else, was reluctant to say goodnight, to go to bed and sleep, as if it were any normal night. They were all on tenterhooks, waiting for the dreaded moment. But they needed sleep. Maria would be sleeping on the couch again tonight, so at least Mario wasn't alone. They all just had to hope that when the sun rose that Mario would wake up too.

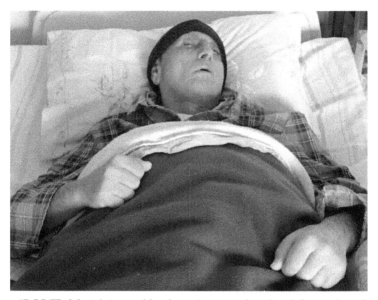

ABOVE: Mario's internal battle continues, weakened and close to the end.

27th August:

With Maria staying in the lounge room for the second night in a row, she had heard how restless Mario had been throughout the night. Calling to her multiple times, she had tended to him much like a mother does to her newborn infant. But his problems couldn't be fixed with a simple feed, burp or cuddle. All Maria could do was be there with him, to let him know that he wasn't alone and she would faithfully keep her vows until the very end.

In sickness and in health.

The sun rose bright, chasing away the shadows on that cold Sunday morning. Mario was still breathing at sunrise, having fought all night to make it to another day. But it was clear that he was reaching the end of his battle. His suffering at its peak. At 6:30am, while the birds sung their song outside to greet a new day, Suzanne gave Mario another dose of morphine for stomach pain. He had another dose only hours later, when Liam came for his daily visit.

'Hi, Mario,' Liam said, even though he was asleep.

'He's not doing well,' Maria said sadly.

Liam looked at Mario. As a nurse, he had been in this situation countless times. He had seen the signs, he had watched patients slip away, surrounded by the sorrow of the family left behind. In his profession, he needed to keep his distance, to remain emotionally detached. But he had a soft spot for Mario. He had appreciated his gentle and kind nature, his beaming smile and bright eyes that welcomed him into their home, and his calm personality that made him an easy patient to care for. Liam had shared cups of tea and homemade nagatales with the family and had been trusted to share the last part of Mario's journey with them. He was saddened to know that he would not be caring for Mario for much longer.

Liam couldn't do much else, but he gently changed Mario's adult diaper. As he did so, he spoke to Mario, telling him what he was doing, as if Mario could hear. When he had finished, he went to wash his hands then came and stood next to Maria.

'Are we approaching the end?' Maria asked, her voice shaky.

He nodded, regretfully. 'I think Mario's on the last stretch now and slipping away. I can't say for sure, though, because it's so hard to predict. And hey, don't forget the 'Mario Factor'. Liam tried to lighten the mood, to take away the look of despair that had settled in Maria's eyes.

After Liam left, Mario kept sleeping. Matthew came over; the rest of his family was coming later. Jordan had taken Emmy home for a couple of hours. The house was quiet. If it had been a normal Sunday morning, it would have been quite peaceful. Even though it was winter, the sun shone outside, a false spring warmth in the air. The weather didn't match what was happening inside. It felt wrong for the sun to be shining so brightly when Mario's light was diminishing. So they stayed indoors, close to Mario. Matthew and Suzanne were reading, every few minutes taking a break to look up at him. It was just past 12:00pm when Mario, eyes still closed, whispered familiar words again.

'Thank you, God.'

Not long after, he uttered those words again.

By early afternoon, the house had filled with the regular family members. Jordan and Emmy were back, and Abbey, Jesaia and Coby had come, as well as Gina and Catena. Luke and Stephanie were there too. Mario continued to sleep. About 2:30pm his eyes shot open and he started squirming. Matthew went over to see if he was okay and Mario looked up at him, his face pinched together.

'I'm so weak. I can't stand it anymore.' His face contorted again, eyes full of pain.

'I know, Dad,' Matthew soothed. 'You've been so brave.'

Mario had another dose of morphine as well as some drops on the tongue to ease his agitation. This sent him back to sleep but only for a short reprieve. Almost two hours later, he woke again, tossing his head from side to side. He mumbled, trying to speak. His speech had worsened and he was now hard to understand.

'I'm sorry, Mario,' Maria apologised. 'I can't understand you.'

He was anxious; frustrated that he couldn't communicate with his family.

'Do you think he is in pain?' Suzanne asked. 'He might be trying to tell us it hurts and we don't know what he is saying.' Panic rose in her chest.

'Maybe we should give him another dose of morphine,' Stephanie suggested.

'We only gave him some two hours ago,' Matthew said, not wanting to pump Mario full of the drug that has a reputation for speeding up death.

'The nurse said it's okay to give it when he needs it. I don't think it can do any more harm. He needs to be comfortable,' Stephanie said.

They decided to give Mario another dose. At 4:20pm, more morphine entered Mario's bloodstream, bringing him down into sleep again.

They had used up all the vials of morphine, so Maria called Liam and he came over to draw up more.

Before Liam left, he told them, 'We are getting closer now. Possibly tonight or tomorrow.'

The afternoon was closing in. Tension was high: palms were sweaty, hearts were racing, cheeks were wet. Everyone was trying to be strong for Mario. The grandfather clock ticked, like a heartbeat. Time moved forward, but was running out. Like the atmospheric pressure that builds before an earthquake, the change could be felt in the air around them. Disaster was closing in. The cracks were visible, now it was just a matter of waiting for the earth-shattering shake that would be the upheaval for them all.

By late afternoon, Luke had left to drive back to Perth. He had hugged Mario and said, 'I won't say goodbye, I'll say see you later…okay, Mario?'

He told Stephanie, 'If there is any change, ring me and I'll come straight back. Stay positive.'

Abbey wanted to take Jesaia and Coby home, away from the impending event. The boys said goodbye to their Nonno one last time, then Abbey leant down so her head was close to Mario's and gave him a heartfelt goodbye.

'Thank you for being such a welcoming and wonderful father-in-law,' she said with a shaky voice. 'I love you, Mario, and look forward to the day when we'll meet again.'

The clock chimed six times, heralding dinnertime. No one wanted to leave Mario's side, so Gina and Catena warmed up some Apricot Chicken and they all ate it around Mario's bedside. They picked at their food; it tasted bland and dry, it stuck in their throat. They ate not because they wanted to, but because they needed energy to get them through what was to come.

Gina and Catena stayed in the kitchen, helping out by cleaning up. Jordan and Emmy were staying the night so he took her and got her ready for bed. As the others moved about the house, trying to act as normally as they could. Mario was surrounded by Maria, Matthew, Suzanne and Stephanie.

The clock struck seven times. The room was dimly lit, allowing them to see Mario's face. They watched him intently, silently. All of a sudden, Stephanie shot forward, leaning closer to Mario. She put her ear close to his face. Listened. Standing straight, she asked, 'Did you hear that? I heard a rattle in his throat!'

Their stomachs dropped. They all turned their ear towards Mario.

'I can't hear anything,' Maria said.

'Neither can I,' admitted Matthew and Suzanne.

'I heard it,' Stephanie said, panicked. She put her head down again and straightened. 'Yep, it's there.'

They stood, holding their breaths, waiting to hear the dreaded rattle. The nurses had told them about the 'death rattle' and said that it was one of the common signs that indicated death was near. The sound comes from the back of the throat, where saliva accumulates in the throat and upper chest.

In the silence, Mario breathed. And then they heard it. A soft rattle as he exhaled.

They looked at each other, eyes wide.

'I heard it too,' Suzanne stammered.

Maria left the lounge room and found Gina.

'Can you please organise for Father Jess to come here? Mario wanted to have a final blessing.'

'I can do that,' Gina said, and reached for her phone.

While they were waiting for Father Jess, Mario's breaths became more laboured. He started breathing faster, trying to take in more oxygen. They took turns to hold his hands, and they noticed they had become clammy.

'He must be feeling hot,' Maria said.

They pulled the blanket and sheet off him, and unbuttoned his pajama top.

The doorbell rang, and Gina answered it. She brought the priest to where the family was and then went back to the kitchen to give them some privacy.

'Hi, Father,' the family said.

'Hello. I'm sorry to hear that Mario is not doing well. I would be honoured to give his final blessing.'

'Thank you for coming at such short notice, Father,' Maria said shakily.

Father Jess sat down beside Mario.

'Hi, Mario. It's nice to see you. I'm going to say a prayer for you now.'

He opened his bible and cleared his throat. Over the sounds of Mario's breathing and rattling, he began to pray the prayer of Commendation:

I commend you, my dear brother,
to almighty God
and entrust you to your Creator.
May you return to Him

who formed you from the dust of the earth.
May holy Mary, the angels, and all the saints
come to meet you as you go forth from this life.
May Christ, who was crucified for you,
bring you freedom and peace.
May Christ, who died for you,
admit you into his garden of paradise.
May Christ, the true Shepherd,
acknowledge you as one of his flock.
May He forgive all your sins
and set you among those He has chosen.
May you see your Redeemer face to face
and enjoy the vision of God for ever.'

He stopped reading and the family responded with an 'Amen.' Father Jess closed his bible and reached into his robe. He pulled out a small container of Holy water, opened the lid and anointed Mario with it.

'Let us pray together the Lord's Prayer.

In unison, voices thick with sorrow, they prayed over Mario.

'Our Father, Who art in heaven
Hallowed be Thy Name;
Thy kingdom come,
Thy will be done,
on earth as it is in heaven.
Give us this day our daily bread,
and forgive us our trespasses,
as we forgive those who trespass against us;
and lead us not into temptation,
but deliver us from evil. Amen.'

They sat in silence for a few moments. Father Jess spoke. 'You know, sometimes it helps to say that it's okay to let go. That you will all be fine. Talk to him; tell him what you're thinking.'

The family paused. Suzanne took a deep breath, leaned closer towards Mario, who had been flitting in and out of consciousness.

'Dad, you know that you don't have to fight anymore, don't you? We will be okay, we'll look after each other.' Tears fell from her face, her words uneven and shaky. 'I'm so proud of you and how you've fought. I'll always hold you in my heart and I'll never forget you.'

Mario looked through foggy eyes at his sobbing daughter.

'Please…don't…cry,' he pleaded. Even on his deathbed, he couldn't bear to see his loved ones in pain.

It was time for Father Jess to leave.

'Goodbye, Mario. God bless you.'

He then spoke to the family. 'You are all in my thoughts. May God give you strength for this next part. Please let me know when Mario passes.'

After Father Jess left, Gina and Catena did too. Emmy was fast asleep on Mario's side of the bed. Tucked away at the back of the house, oblivious that her Nonno was dying not far from her. Jordan joined the family, taking a seat on the couch.

Around 8:30pm, things started to intensify even more. The rattle in Mario's throat couldn't be mistaken now. The gurgle was loud and unpleasant and it sounded like he was choking. Medical professionals say that it is more distressing for the people listening to it than it is for the person dying. The family certainly hoped this was true.

Mario mumbled something. Everyone looked at each other.

'What did he say?' Suzanne asked.

'I think he said, "I saw an angel", but I can't be sure,' Matthew answered.

'Oh…wow,' Suzanne breathed, wishing they could all see what Mario was seeing and know how he was feeling.

Mario started to become very agitated, tossing his head back and forth.

'I…want some…apple…juice,' Mario gasped.

'Did he just say he wants a drink?' Maria asked hopefully. The desperate thought ran through all their minds: if he wanted a drink, maybe it was a sign he would pick up. Clinging to any bit of hope, they wanted it to be true. If he could drink, then maybe it wasn't as bad as it seemed.

'Let's get him some then,' Maria said.

'But how will he drink it? What if he chokes?' Stephanie questioned. She was right, he wasn't in any state to drink.

'I know!' Matthew said. He poured some apple juice into a cup and with a cotton swab, dabbed the liquid onto Mario's parched lips. 'Here you go, Dad.'

Mario turned his face away. Matthew followed and continued to dab softly. Mario scrunched his face up, and turned away again, a look of annoyance crossing his face.

'Please, Matthew,' Mario pleaded. 'Stop forcing me!'

Matthew's hand shot back.

'Oh, Dad. I'm sorry. I thought you wanted a drink.'

They all felt bad for mistaking what he had wanted. They all felt disappointed, their false hope dashed. Mario continued to moan and groan, writhing frantically on the bed. The family hovered over him, feeling helpless. Mario wasn't alone but he had to face death alone – he couldn't express fully what he was feeling, he couldn't tell his family about the emotions he was experiencing, or the state of his mind. He was staring death in the face and only he knew what that looked like.

Mario turned his head towards the grandfather clock. He saw Maria and Stephanie on that side. He turned his head the other way, and could see Matthew and Suzanne.

'Darling,' he cried out. 'Put the book away, I think I'm dying!'

He saw their faces, pinched with worry, with fear, with sadness. He couldn't bear their pain on top of his.

'Please be positive,' he encouraged.

The walls were closing in on him. The space became smaller and the air became harder to breathe. Why was his family just standing there?

'Please,' he begged. 'Why aren't you helping me?'

Their faces hovered over his. Their hands touched him. Their mouths moved but he couldn't understand.

'Darling…you're not doing much about it.'

Mario started gasping for air. His mouth opened wide as he took rapid, long breaths. Like a fish out of water, he snapped at the air, trying to suck in oxygen.

Everyone started to panic, distraught at seeing Mario struggling for air.

Matthew turned to Jordan. 'Can you please call Liam? We don't know what to do.'

Jordan hopped up straight away, going into the next room to find Liam's number. He went outside and made the call. A couple minutes later he came back in.

'Liam suggested to give Mario some space. He said if you're all surrounding him it could be quite overwhelming for him. He also suggested playing some music, which might help him to relax.'

They sprang into action. Suzanne and Stephanie moved to the couch, their hands shaking as they watched their Dad struggle. Matthew found a song that he had played for Mario over the last few weeks. He put the phone near the bed and sat on the other couch. As *Amazing Grace* started to fill the space, Maria sat beside Mario and held his hand. Before long, Mario's breaths became less rapid and he seemed to calm down. His eyes stared at a point in the ceiling, like he was transfixed by something there.

'It's okay, Mario,' Maria soothed. 'I'm here. You're doing so well. You've been so brave.' She stroked his hand and stared into his eyes. She followed his gaze up to the ceiling.

'What can you see, Mario?' she asked, not expecting an answer.

Then, just like that, Mario's breaths became laboured again. His agitation returned in full force.

'Oh Mario! It wasn't supposed to be this hard for you,' she cried. 'You can stop fighting, Mario. Just let go.' Her tears fell like rain.

'Matthew, can you call Liam again?'

Matthew stopped the music, picked up his phone and dialled Liam's number. As Matthew spoke, Mario's breaths slowed down. His gasps became short, with longer pauses in between. His large, swollen stomach heaved up, then down.

'Oh, Mario!' Maria sobbed.

Mario focused on Maria's face: the face of his Darling, who he had loved forever. The face of the woman who had cared for him throughout their whole marriage. Who had given him three children and raised them. Who had been there throughout it all, even in their hardest of times. He was staring into the face of the strongest woman he knew, the one who had granted him his wish to die at home. He looked at his Darling as a tear fell from his eye.

Another gasp. A longer pause between breaths. Stomach rises, then falls.

This was it. His moment was here. He had to let go. Mario summoned the fighting spirit within him and gathered enough strength to give his Darling one last gift. He looked directly into her eyes and smiled at her. Silently, with his eyes he spoke: *Goodbye, Darling.*

In the background, Matthew was still on the phone to Liam but with one ear listening to what was happening in the lounge room.

Mario drew in another quick breath. The pause went on.

'Mario!' Maria called.

Suzanne and Stephanie jumped up from the chair and rushed over. They were sobbing hysterically.

'Is he gone?' Suzanne asked.

'I think so,' Maria cried.

At the same time, Matthew saw what was happening. Cutting Liam off mid-conversation, he said, 'Liam, I have to go. I think he has passed.'

As Matthew disconnected the call and ran over, Mario took one last gasp. They waited for another breath but it didn't come. Mario's eyes remained open. Lifeless eyes stared blankly at the ceiling. His mouth hung open, but breathed no air. Maria, Matthew, Suzanne and Stephanie threw themselves on him, resting their heads on his stomach and chest. Their cries filled the room, a chorus of sorrow as they held onto Mario and grieved their loss.

'He's actually gone,' Suzanne lamented.

'I can't believe it,' Stephanie sobbed.

'What's the time?' Matthew asked, grief lacing his question.

Their eyes moved to the grandfather clock above them.

'10:45pm,' Suzanne said.

Jordan came and hugged each of them, sharing in their pain. They all sat down beside Mario and stared at him. They were numb with shock and disbelief. It was over. Ever since his diagnosis they had been waiting for this moment, unsure of when it would be. Now it was here and they couldn't quite wrap their heads around it. Mario was gone. They felt empty and hollow. The heartache was raw. A piece of them had been taken away the moment Mario took his last breath. They sat in silence, as their brains tried to comprehend what had just occurred. This morning he was here. He could see, feel, hear and touch. His heart pumped, his lungs breathed. Now, he lay unmoving, eternally sleeping. His face, which used to be a window into his soul, was expressionless. That bright smile that made his eyes shine too was an image that only their memory could bring back to life.

Matthew broke the silence. 'I guess we better call a doctor to come and certify Dad's death.'

On one of the visits from the palliative nurses, they had discussed the procedure about what they would need to do if Mario passed away outside of working hours. They had been given an after-hours number; it had been written on a card, ready for when the time came.

Jordan rose from his chair. 'I'll do that.'

The call was re-directed to Dr Dorkham, who happened to be the doctor on call that night. He was just about to go to bed, but instead of putting his pajamas on and hopping into bed he put his work clothes on and hopped in his car.

While they were waiting for the doctor to arrive, Stephanie called Luke and told him the news. Jordan called Tony to let him know that Mario had passed away and asked him if he could let the rest of the family know. Maria stayed by Mario's side. She stood up and gently closed Mario's eyes with her fingertips. His right eye didn't close properly, even after she had tried a number of times. It had closed half way but was slit open slightly, his unseeing eye visible beneath his eyelashes. It was disconcerting; if he had both eyes fully closed they could have just pretended he was asleep.

'Oh,' Maria said. 'He already feels cold.'

About 11:30pm Dr Dorkham's car headlights flooded the driveway. In the stillness of night, they heard the engine turn off, the door close and then his footsteps as he came up the stairs to knock on the door. Jordan greeted him and let him into the house.

The family's hellos were solemn and Dr Dorkham approached with a sympathetic look on his face.

'I'm sorry for your loss,' he said. 'What time did Mario pass?'

Maria cleared her throat. '10:45pm,' she answered.

Dr Dorkham respectively examined Mario and as expected, found no signs of life. He filled out a form then asked, 'Are you having Mario's body collected tonight?'

'No,' Matthew said. 'We'll organise that tomorrow.'

'That's no problem.' He paused and then pointed to Mario's face. 'Were you wanting to close Mario's mouth? If you were it would need to be done soon. It doesn't take long for the muscles to stiffen. Once that happens there's no way you'll be able to close it.'

'Oh,' Maria said. 'Yes, I'd like his mouth closed.' Her voice was thick with grief.

'Would you like me to do it?' Dr Dorkham asked.

'Yes please,' Maria said, nodding.

Dr Dorkham walked closer to Mario and gently placed his fingers on Mario's chin. He pushed upwards and held his mouth in position for a few seconds and then he let go. Mario's mouth dropped open immediately. He tried again, but Mario's mouth flopped open.

'Have you got a towel?'

Jordan went to the linen cupboard and retrieved a towel. Dr Dorkham rolled it up and placed it in the nook between Mario's chin and chest. This pushed Mario's mouth closed and held it in position.

'There. Keep the towel like that overnight.'

The family thanked him. Dr Dorkham picked up his bag, getting ready to leave.

'I'm sorry again. Please look after yourselves.'

Jordan saw him out and they all took their places back by Mario's bedside. The clock had struck midnight; they were mentally, emotionally and physically exhausted but yet they felt wide-awake, the adrenalin still coursing through their veins.

'Should we have a cuppa in honour of Dad?' Matthew suggested.

They nodded, tears filling their eyes, remembering how much Mario enjoyed his cups of tea.

Jordan boiled the kettle. 'Can you please make one for Mario? Use his mug,' Maria asked.

'Of course,' Jordan answered and set about making everyone a cup of tea.

Jordan set Mario's hot cup of tea on a chair beside him, in the mug he had used daily. Once everyone had their drink in their hands, they toasted Mario.

'To Dad,' Matthew said. 'He's in a better place now.'

'To your Fighting Spirit. You put up a good fight, Dad,' Suzanne said, as she tasted the bitterness of her tears.

'And we're so proud of you,' Stephanie added.

They all nodded, looking at Mario and raising their mugs. They brought their drinks to their mouths, taking a sip. But without Mario, it just didn't taste the same.

While they were drinking, they heard another car pull up in the driveway. Then the sound of footsteps running up the stairs. Jordan opened the door and let the visitor inside. Everyone turned to see who it was. Stephanie jumped up when she saw it was Luke. They embraced; held onto each other without saying anything for a moment. Luke was out of breath, his hands shaking as he held Stephanie.

'I'm sorry I wasn't here. As soon as you called me I got straight back in my car and drove down. I shouldn't have left in the first place.'

'Thanks for coming back,' Stephanie said.

With Luke now by their side too, they spent some more time with Mario. As it got later, Matthew stood.

'Sorry, Mum, but I better get home. I'll come back first thing in the morning.'

Matthew leant down and hugged Mario, as if it was just a normal goodbye.

'Goodnight, Dad,' he whispered, as he kissed his cold forehead.

Once Matthew had gone, it was time for the others to start thinking about getting ready for bed. They didn't want to leave Mario, but their weariness was starting to set in. Stephanie and Luke went first, then Jordan. Suzanne sat with her Dad while Maria showered. Now alone, she sat next to him, trying to recall his smile, and the way he used to look at her. Her mind replayed the night, and how they had watched him fighting for air. Wanting a better image as a memory, she tried to picture the way he hugged her every time they saw each other. She pulled the blanket down and buttoned up his pajama top, then tucked him back in. Tenderly, she put her hand to his icy forehead and tried to remember the warmth of his skin. The clock continued to tick; it seemed louder now there was no other noises to drown out the sound. Life without Mario had begun. With a heavy heart, Suzanne kissed him goodnight.

'I love you, Dad,' she murmured. 'See you in the morning.'

While the rest of the family tried to sleep, Maria stayed up a while longer, sitting and staring at her lifeless husband. Numb with shock and heavy with grief, the burden of her loss was crushing. After some time, she forced herself to get up. With only a few hours until the sun rose, she turned the lights off, putting the house in darkness. She couldn't bear to leave Mario alone, so she resumed her spot on the couch.

Tomorrow would be the beginning of a new week. Tomorrow the sun would bring light, but to Mario's family, the world would be a little darker, for Mario was no longer in it.

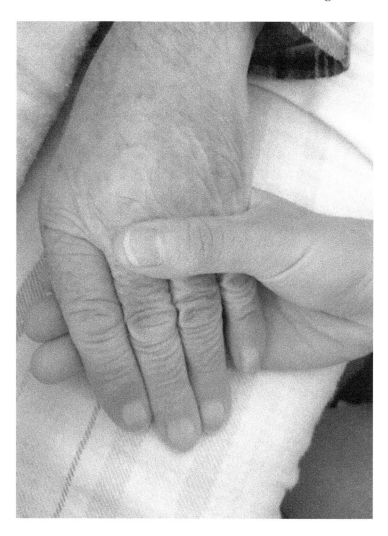

ABOVE: Suzanne holds onto Mario, even though he is gone.

29

Grief in Letting Go

The next morning, everyone woke early, still in a daze. The weather outside held the promise of spring; the sky was clear, except for a splattering of fluffy white clouds here and there. The air was chilly, the slight breeze carrying the birds' joyous song through the open door. It was as if the birds could feel spring in the air and they wanted everyone to know it. Winter was nearly over. Flowers would soon bloom, trees would grow new leaves, birds would build nests and new life would be created. The weather was preparing to celebrate the emergence of renewal and life, and yet, for Mario's family, they were in the depths of grief.

No one quite knew what to do with themselves; they moved slowly, as if in a trance, and spoke with a tremor in their voices. Jordan quickly got Emmy and himself ready, and left to go back to their house. The others, in their own time, went into the lounge to see Mario. They sat beside him and ate their breakfast, still keeping him a part of their usual routine. Matthew came over and it wasn't long before other family members appeared at the house to give their condolences and to see Mario for the last time. The driveway filled up quickly, and each time someone new entered the house, fresh tears were shed. On Mario's side there was his brother, Frank and his wife, Antoinette, Robbie and Angie, and Tony and Wendy. On Maria's side there was Gina and Catena, her brother Vince and his partner, Debbie, and two of her other brothers, Frank and Angelo. There were no words that would ease the pain, but their support was appreciated. Their visit allowed them to give a final goodbye to Mario, and once everyone had had a chance to do that, they left.

Now, with the house quiet again, Maria, Matthew, Suzanne, Stephanie and Luke could focus on what needed to be done next.

'I'll call Liam to find out what he needs to do,' Matthew said. 'Then I'll call Archer's to ask them to pick Dad up. What time do you want them to come?'

Maria paused, reluctant to let go. She looked at the clock.

'Um…let's have a few more hours. Can you ask them to come at 12:00pm?'

'Will do,' Matthew answered, and left the room to make the calls. Around mid-morning, Liam arrived. He gave his condolences to the family and looked sadly at Mario. He approached his patient and said warmly, 'Hi Mario.' He then asked the family about the events of the night before and shakily, they told them how it had all happened.

'You guys did such a great job,' Liam encouraged. 'It's not easy caring for a loved one who is dying, but you gave him his wish to die at home. You should all be very proud of yourselves.'

Maria's eyes were glistening with tears. She began to speak, and they spilled over. 'He seemed so distressed. I didn't think it would be like that. I've heard that it can be quick, that they can slip away in their sleep, but Mario was gasping for breath.'

Liam listened, sympathetic to the pain Maria was expressing.

'Every death is different and there's no way to predict how each one will go, but that is the natural process of dying. You were there right until the end, Maria, and that would have reassured him very much.'

Maria wiped her tears, and Liam explained that he needed to take out the port. He turned back and as if Mario could hear, said, 'I'm going to take your port out now.' He worked gently and respectfully. When he had finished, he collected the medication box that had been left at the house.

'Okay, guys, I'll leave you now.'

They all thanked him for taking such good care of Mario. Before Liam left, he told the family, 'You should be so proud of how you looked after Mario. I can see how much you all love each other. Thank you for being so welcoming every time I visited. You know, it's a rare thing to have such a close knit family and I must admit, I'm kind of jealous of what you have.'

It was getting close to 12:00pm. Maria, Matthew, Suzanne and Stephanie had been sitting with Mario since Liam left. None of them were ready for Mario to be taken away; sitting next to his lifeless, cold body was better than not having him there at all.

They took turns holding his hand. Maria put his wedding ring on and took a photo. When they heard the car pull up in the driveway, their stomachs did a somersault. Matthew went out to greet the undertakers and they told him to take their time. They would bring the car up the back and get the stretcher ready and wait for their signal to come inside.

One by one the family said their final goodbyes to Mario, putting their arms over him and kissing him on the head.

'Goodbye, Mario. I hope you're at peace now. I love you,' Maria sobbed.

'Dad, I'm so proud of you. I can't wait to see you again someday,' Matthew cried.

Suzanne went next. 'I'll never forget you, Dad. I'll always try to make you proud. And I promise I'll finish your book, so that everyone will know your fighting spirit.'

'Goodbye, Dad. You fought so hard and we're all so proud of you. You're the strongest person I know,' Stephanie said through tears.

Matthew then motioned for Peter and Bob to come inside. Pulling the stretcher, they entered the house slowly and quietly. Peter took Maria's hand and offered his condolences. He was a softly spoken man, with a gentle, warm voice. His presence was calming; he had a kind, genuine energy and spoke with empathy and care.

'When you're ready, Maria, we will carefully lift Mario onto the stretcher.'

The family stood united, their shared grief like a rising storm. After some time, Maria nodded and ever so carefully, Peter and Bob, with Matthew's help, slowly lifted Mario onto the stretcher. Maria's sobs filled the room, her breaths fast and panicked.

'He didn't want to ever leave this house,' she wailed.

Her children held her up, pillars to stop her from crumbling to the ground. She cried like she hadn't before, the sounds of her heart shattering into pieces. She started spluttering; she was still unwell with her persistent cough.

'Sit down, Mum,' Matthew said, and they sat her down on a chair.

'Breathe,' Suzanne soothed. 'Try to calm down.'

Maria coughed some more and cried some more. Then she took a deep breath, composed herself and said, 'I'm okay.'

She stood up shakily, and stood next to the stretcher. She looked at Mario for a moment longer. 'Okay,' she said.

Bob and Peter pulled the sheet over Mario's feet. They brought it up slowly, and the family kept their eyes trained on Mario's face, ingraining his features into their minds. Tears wet their cheeks as the sheet was pulled over his face, and he was hidden from their view. Bob and Peter started wheeling the stretcher outside. The family trailed behind, watching as the stretcher was placed into the car, their arms linked and hearts aching.

Suzanne noticed the make of the car. 'Look, it's a Holden.'

Maria gave a small smile, thinking of Mario's love of the cars. 'He would be happy that he's getting a ride in a Commodore.'

'Lucky it's not a Ford, he wouldn't be too impressed his last ride was in a Ford,' Matthew joked.

The family laughed, brief and fleeting, but it helped ease the pain for a second.

Once Mario was safely and securely in the car, they closed the boot. Peter came over to Maria and took her hands again. 'I'm very sorry, Maria. We'll be in touch soon to discuss the funeral arrangements. Please don't hesitate to call if you need anything.'

'Thank you,' Maria said, her lip quivering.

They got into the car, started the engine and slowly started inching their way out of the narrow driveway. The family stood rooted to the spot, watching the car pull away. Watching as Mario was taken away from the house that he had built with his own hands, and from the people he had cherished and loved dearly. His existence was now just a memory that lived in their hearts and minds.

30

Time to Say Goodbye

The following week, on the 5th of September, Mario's family prepared to give their final farewell. The intervening week had been spent organising the details of his funeral. Thankfully, Mario had had a chance to express his wishes beforehand, so it was just a matter of putting it all together, to create the send-off he had requested.

It was early spring and already there was warmth in the air. The sky was bright blue, the earth green and vibrant after the winter rain. It was an otherwise perfect day, except for the fact that they would be burying Mario.

Matthew and Suzanne met Maria and Stephanie at the house. They inhaled deeply and looked at each other.

'Let's go,' Matthew said.

First they huddled together with heads touching and arms around each other, like a team does before a big game. Matthew prayed for strength to get through the day, and for them to find peace when their hearts were aching.

'Amen,' they said in unison.

With a deep sigh, Suzanne looked to her family. 'Let's do this.'

The funeral was at St Patrick's at 1:00pm. They arrived at 12:30pm and stood outside the church, waiting for Archers. Other family members started to congregate and offered their condolences before entering the church.

Hearing the soft purr of an engine, they turned and saw the hearse approaching. As it pulled up in front of the church, they had a full view of Mario's coffin through the clear windows. The proximity to Mario was overwhelming. So close, but yet so far away. It was a morbid thought, but they wondered what he looked like, a week after his death. They tried to imagine him in his black suit, his hands clasped over his rosary beads. He would have his crucifix necklace visible over his white shirt, and his engagement and wedding ring on his left hand. Surrounding him was his Bible, his copy of Fighting Spirit and pictures that Jesaia, Coby and Emmy had drawn for him.

Peter came around to greet Maria and the family. He wore the same empathetic expression on his face.

'How are you holding up, Maria?'

'I'm...okay,' she said, looking past Peter at the hearse, her face crumpling.

Peter patted her arm, a silent acknowledgement of understanding.

He spoke quietly and explained what would happen next.

Peter then gathered the pallbearers and explained what they needed to do. Carefully, they slid the coffin out and lifted it onto the funeral trolley. After they had it positioned securely, they wheeled it through the doors of the church. Maria and Matthew stood behind the coffin, and Suzanne and Stephanie stood behind them. Father Jess took his place at the front. On the right side stood Ron, Tony and Frank and on the left stood Brian, Robbie and Armando. They all waited for the sound of the music that would accompany their entry into the church. Matthew linked arms with Maria,

Suzanne with Stephanie. When they heard the beginning notes of music floating through the air, they took a deep breath and prepared themselves for an emotional few hours. As their hearts pounded in time with the music, they moved forward.

Amazing Grace, how sweet the sound…

The swell of sweet singing filled the church as they entered into a sea of black, the people in their pews turning to see Mario's coffin slowly being wheeled forward.

I once was lost, but now I'm found…

Maria, Matthew, Suzanne and Stephanie stared straight ahead, not daring to make eye contact with any of the faces that stared sadly at them. The music stirred their hearts and brought their sorrow to the surface. They had played this song to Mario when he had been bedridden. He had listened with a soft smile, the music filling his soul and stirring his own emotions. His heart held the hope of Heaven, his faith never wavering even in his darkest days.

God's grace has brought me safely here, and grace will lead me home…

They were almost at the front of the church. Mario's family could only accompany him so far; they finally had to leave him and take their seats. As powerless as they had been to ease Mario's pain, so too were they unable to walk with him any longer. Hard as it was to say goodbye, they could take comfort knowing that his suffering had ended.

My chains are gone, I've been set free…

Once they and the pallbearers were seated, the final notes of the song played out and a moment of silence gave pause to the proceedings, before Father Jess stood and gave the introductory rites. He sprinkled Holy Water over and placed the Baptismal Pall on the coffin and gave the opening prayer.

Mario had wanted a traditional Catholic mass and so the service included the Liturgy of the Word, Homily, Prayers of the Faithful, Liturgy of the Eucharist, and the Rites of Communion. This was followed by a much more personal tribute. Tony, Matthew, Suzanne and Stephanie each stood at the pulpit, their eyes sweeping over the congregation while they offered their words of remembrance. Voices broke and tears were shed as they spoke from the heart; talking about the wonderful qualities that Mario possessed, how strong and brave and inspirational he was, how loved and respected he was.

Then the large screen on the wall lit up and everyone watched a pictorial tribute to Mario. As his face filled the screen and images of his smiling face looked out at everybody, once again many reached for their tissues as they relived snippets of Mario's life.

Father Jess then gave the Final Commendation and Final Blessing. Maria, Matthew, Suzanne and Stephanie stood, as well as the pallbearers, taking their place at Mario's coffin again. Music filled the room once more, and as *How Great Thou Art* played, they walked out of the church and made their way to Bunbury Lawn Cemetery.

As the mid-afternoon sun shone high in the sky, family and friends stood around Mario's open grave. Father Jess prayed and before they knew it, Maria, Matthew, Suzanne and Stephanie were standing beside Mario's coffin, ready to bid the final farewell. As *Time to Say Goodbye* played, they watched Mario's coffin being slowly lowered into the ground. They held onto each other, as their cries echoed around them, a haunting sound of grief that came from the depths of their souls. Once the coffin gently rested on the earth, one by one they released a red rose from their hand, and watched it fall through blurry eyes, onto the wooden lid. Others came with handfuls of lavender to throw into the grave, arm outstretched as they added to the symbolic gesture: their last sign of respect and the hope that Mario would start a new life after death.

The family remained by Mario's grave as people came to express their condolences. Eventually, people started to leave until there was just Mario's immediate family. In the quiet, noises that couldn't before be heard now became amplified. The whoosh of cars in the distance. The rustle of leaves as a slight breeze blew. Birds calling to each other, chirping and singing joyfully. Signs that the world continued even in times of despair. That life moved on and seasons changed. That even when the heart ached and yearned for a loved one, there was always hope.

It was time for them to leave Mario. They needed to head back to the house to hold the wake, which would take place in Mario's beloved shed, surrounded by his tools and his handiwork. They would mourn the loss of Mario but also celebrate his life. Before they turned to leave, they paused by the grave, reflecting on the special man they loved.

With Mario's passing, they had only lost their physical connection to him. Ingrained in their blood, his fighting spirit coursed through their veins, and in that way, he lived on. In that way, he would have immortality.

Scan this QR code to watch a video tribute to the life of Mario.

Or visit:

www.suzifaed.com/tribute/

ABOVE: The pallbearers pull Mario's coffin out of the car, St Patrick's Church, 5th September, 2017.

ABOVE: The pallbearers, from front left – Ron, Tony and Frank, from front right – Brian, Robbie and Armando.

LEFT: Mario's resting place, Bunbury Lawn Cemetery, 5th September, 2017.

Epilogue

In the lead up to Dad's death, when he looked back on his life, amazingly, he said he had no regrets. If he could have had his time over again, he wouldn't have changed anything. He would go through it all again, believing that all the trials he had faced made him appreciate life more, made him stronger and more mature. He had never travelled, other than his voyage to Australia and to a few country towns in the small pocket of the South West. Dad was content with that, never desiring to be anywhere other than with his family.

Some people spend their lives never quite satisfied with the hand they have been dealt. Always searching for more money, more experiences, things that will fill them up and make them feel less empty. Dad didn't need any of that; family and faith was of more value to him than all the possessions in the world. Religion had always been important to Dad; he always had a strong faith, unwavering even in the darkest moments of his life. He believed in the promise of Heaven; sure that he would be in God's arms when his time on earth was done.

Dad's greatest wish was to have lived a good life. That it wasn't wasted on superficial things, but with qualities that showed the goodness of a loving heart: to be honest, caring, truthful and respectful. Dad proved, throughout his life, that he was all this and more.

This man, my Dad, was often misunderstood. I spent years misunderstanding him. I saw him through a child's eyes; black and white and uninformed. I took his illness personally, always thinking about how it affected me and not him. Now, my eyes are open to the man he was before he left us: kind, caring, loving, understanding, loyal, humble, authentic, positive and brave. So incredibly brave.

It has been an honour to unmask his history and give his story a voice. He existed on this planet, he lived and laughed and loved and lost. But most importantly, he fought. He fought for the precious thing that is life, his journey long and hard in places, but a journey worth every minute. A man who lived for his family, and showed them what it really means to have a fighting spirit.

After I finished writing about Dad's life prior to his death, he read the rough manuscript, thanked me and said he was happy to know his story had been penned, a memoir for the family to keep and reminisce over. I promised him that I would continue his story until the very end and that I would get it published so that people wouldn't forget. I hope that I have done justice in documenting his life and in highlighting the main message of this book: behind an ordinary man lived an extraordinary existence. That his outside appearance, made weak from his many health issues, did not reflect the man he was inside. The spirit of a true warrior lived within him. His inner strength, his willpower and resolve to never give up, no matter what, was an inspiration to many.

It was clear he was pleased; that his life meant enough to somebody to spend the time to have it documented, a piece of him kept in history, his presence on this earth validated.

We will remember my Dad for being normal, for being kind and caring, for having a heart big enough to show that all you really need is love. We will remember him for all that, plus so much more. His story could have been lost, along with his essence and fighting spirit. It could have been lost, if no one had sat down with him and asked him that long overdue question: When you look back on your life, what do you want to be remembered for?

I am just thankful that I finally asked.

ABOVE: Mario's gravestone,
Bunbury Lawn Cemetery, 8ᵗʰ June, 2018.

Acknowledgements

I would like to acknowledge a number of people who have assisted me throughout the writing of this biography. I have very much appreciated their advice, input, and time spent helping me make this book a reality.

A massive thank you to the following:

To Jill, for editing my manuscript to a higher standard by combing through each page to untangle the sentences that needed re-writing. For your 'comma-queen' ability, for tidying up my punctuation and grammar, and for eliminating words that are in my vocabulary, but not the dictionary's.

To Ian Andrew, for exposing me to the concept of independent publishing. Also for assisting with the various aspects of the formatting and publishing process, as well as generously editing my manuscript and providing me with great advice.

To Nicole, for offering your time and reading through the first few chapters. Thank you for providing me with suggestions on re-wording certain parts, and contributing further information on some areas of Dad's life.

To Cilla, for editing the proof copy – The Final Edit! Thanks for kindly giving of your time to help me. I'm sorry you also know the pain of losing a father, but through that loss we are connected.

To everyone who opened up their photo albums to provide me with snapshots of Dad's life: especially Mum and Dad, Tony and Matthew.

Also, I can't close without acknowledging my loving family who have supported, encouraged and believed I could finish this project that is so very close to my heart.

First and foremost to Dad, for being so willing to talk about your life, and sharing the parts that would much rather be forgotten. How I treasure those hours spent talking to you and listening to your stories. Your strength still inspires me.

Thank you, Jordan, for allowing me the time and space to write and for putting up with the emotional rollercoaster that often ensued after a writing session. Especially after Dad was gone and writing was especially difficult. Sometimes it was like re-opening fresh wounds, so I appreciate your patience and understanding.

Finally, from my heart, I thank you, Mum. Although this story was about Dad, you were at the heart of it too. You faithfully and selflessly looked after Dad and remained strong for your family. I so admire your inner strength and resilience. Thank you for all you have done over the years, and continue to do. You truly are a warrior and have the Fighting Spirit within you too.

You will always be Dad's special Darling.

About the Author

Suzanne Faed is a wife, a full-time mother to an energetic, book-loving little girl, a qualified teacher, and a writer.

She graduated from Edith Cowan University, Mount Lawley, with a Bachelor of Arts in Writing and a Diploma of Education in Early Childhood Studies, having taught pre-primary before the birth of her daughter.

Suzanne's father suffered from a mental illness, and this had a significant impact on her childhood. She always used writing as a way to explore her feelings, and it was this self-expression that led to her love of writing and using her experiences to inspire her work.

Her debut picture book, *My Daddy is Different*, will be published by Empowering Resources and explores, through the eyes of a child, the impact of having a parent with a mental illness.

Living in the coastal city of Bunbury, Western Australia, Suzanne enjoys being close to the beach. Her interests include reading, playing volleyball and tennis, kayaking, boxing and, most importantly, spending time with her family.

She can be followed online or through social media:

Website: www.suzifaed.com

Facebook: www.facebook.com/suzifaedauthor/

Instagram: www.instagram.com/suzifaedauthor/

Email at: suzifaedauthor@gmail.com

Seeking Help

If mental health or cancer issues have affected you or any of your family or friends, you can contact:

Mental Health – Helplines:
Lifeline Australia: 13 11 14
Beyond Blue: 1300 22 4636
Headspace – National Office: (03) 9027 0100
Kids Helpline: 1800 55 1800
SANE Australia: 1800 187 263

Mental Health – Resources:
Lifeline Australia: https://www.lifeline.org.au
Beyond Blue: https://www.beyondblue.org.au
Headspace: https://headspace.org.au
Kids Helpline: https://kidshelpline.com.au
SANE Australia: https://www.sane.org

Cancer – Helplines:
Cancer Council: 13 11 20
Bowel Cancer Australia: 1800 555 494
Canteen: 1800 835 932
Cancer Australia: 1800 624 973

Cancer – Resources:
Cancer Council: https://www.cancer.org.au
Bowel Cancer Australia: https://www.bowelcanceraustralia.org
Canteen: https://www.canteen.org.au
Cancer Australia: https://canceraustralia.gov.au

www.ingramcontent.com/pod-product-compliance
Ingram Content Group Australia Pty Ltd
76 Discovery Rd, Dandenong South VIC 3175, AU
AUHW020639050325
407891AU00002B/3